Euripides.
Iphigeneia in Tauris. Translated by
Richmond Lattimore. New York, Oxford
University Press, 1973.
x, 88 p.
(The Greek tragedy in new translations)

Translation of Iphigenia Taurica.

I.Lattimore, Richmond Alexander, 1906-
tr. II.Title

D1060319

THE GREEK TRAGEDY
IN NEW TRANSLATIONS

GENERAL EDITOR   William Arrowsmith

EURIPIDES: **Iphigeneia in Tauris**

EURIPIDES

Iphigeneia in Tauris

Translated by
RICHMOND LATTIMORE

OXFORD UNIVERSITY PRESS
New York and London
1973

Printed in the United States of America

To Mabel Lang

EDITOR'S FOREWORD

The Greek Tragedy in New Translations is based on the conviction that poets like Aeschylus, Sophocles, and Euripides can only be properly rendered by translators who are themselves poets. Scholars may, it is true, produce useful and perceptive versions. But our most urgent present need is for a *re-creation* of these plays—as though they had been written, freshly and greatly, by masters fully at home in the English of our own times. Unless the translator is a poet, his original is likely to reach us in crippled form: deprived of the power and pertinence it must have if it is to speak to us of what is permanent in the Greek. But poetry is not enough; the translator must obviously know what he is doing, or he is bound to do it badly. Clearly, few contemporary poets possess enough Greek to undertake the complex and formidable task of transplanting a Greek play without also "colonializing" it or stripping it of its deep cultural difference, its remoteness from us. And that means depriving the play of that crucial *otherness* of Greek experience—a quality no less valuable to us than its closeness. Collaboration between scholar and poet is therefore the essential operating principle of the series. In fortunate cases scholar and poet co-exist; elsewhere we have teamed able poets and scholars in an effort to supply, through affinity and intimate collaboration, the necessary combination of skills.

An effort has been made to provide the general reader or student with first-rate critical introductions, clear expositions of translators' principles, commentary on difficult passages, ample stage directions, and glossaries of mythical and geographical terms encountered in the plays. Our purpose throughout has been to make the reading of the plays as vivid as possible. But our poets have constantly tried to remember that they were translating *plays*—plays meant to be produced, in language that actors could speak, naturally and with dignity. The poetry aims at being *dramatic* poetry and realizing itself in words and actions that are both speakable and playable.

Finally, the reader should perhaps be aware that no pains have been spared in order that the "minor" plays should be translated as carefully and brilliantly as the acknowledged masterpieces. For the Greek Tragedy in New Translations aims to be, in the fullest sense, *new*. If we need vigorous new poetic versions, we also need to see the plays with fresh eyes, to reassess the plays *for ourselves*, in terms of our own needs. This means translations that liberate us from the canons of an earlier age because the translators have recognized, and discovered, in often neglected works, the perceptions and wisdom that make these works ours and necessary to us.

A NOTE ON THE SERIES FORMAT

If only for the illusion of coherence, a series of thirty-three Greek plays requires a consistent format. Different translators, each with his individual voice, cannot possibly develop the sense of a single coherent style for each of the three tragedians; nor even the illusion that, despite their differences, the tragedians share a common set of conventions and a generic, or period, style. But they can at least share a common approach to orthography and a common vocabulary of conventions.

1. *Spelling of Greek Names*
Adherence to the old convention whereby Greek names were first Latinized before being housed in English is gradually disappearing. We are now clearly moving away from Latinization and toward precise transliteration. The break with tradition may be regrettable, but there is much to be said for hearing and seeing Greek names as though they were both *Greek and new*, instead of Roman or neo-classical importations. We cannot of course see them as wholly new. For better or worse certain names and myths are too deeply rooted in our literature and thought to be dislodged. To speak of "Helene" and "Hekabe" would be no less pedantic and absurd than to write "Aischylos" or "Platon" or "Thoukydides." There are of course borderline cases.

"Jocasta" (as opposed to "Iokaste") is not a major mythical figure in her own right; her familiarity in her Latin form is a function of the fame of Sophocles' play as the tragedy *par excellence*. And as tourists we go to Delphi, not Delphoi. The precisely transliterated form may be pedantically "right," but the pedantry goes against the grain of cultural habit and actual usage.

As a general rule, we have therefore adopted a "mixed" orthography according to the principles suggested above. When a name has been firmly housed in English (admittedly the question of domestication is often moot), the traditional spelling has been kept. Otherwise names have been transliterated. Throughout the series the -os termination of masculine names has been adopted, and Greek diphthongs (as in Iphigeneia) have normally been retained. We cannot expect complete agreement from readers (or from translators, for that matter) about borderline cases. But we want at least to make the operative principle clear: to walk a narrow line between orthographical extremes in the hope of keeping what should not, if possible, be lost; and refreshing, in however tenuous a way, the specific sound and name-boundedness of Greek experience.

2. *Stage directions*

The ancient manuscripts of the Greek plays do not supply stage directions (though the ancient commentators often provide information relevant to staging, delivery, "blocking," etc.). Hence stage directions must be inferred from words and situations and our knowledge of Greek theatrical conventions. At best this is a ticklish and uncertain procedure. But it is surely preferable that good stage directions should be provided by the translator than that the reader should be left to his own devices in visualizing action, gesture, and spectacle. Obviously the directions supplied should be both spare and defensible. Ancient tragedy was austere and "distanced" by means of masks, which means that the reader must not expect the detailed intimacy ("He shrugs and turns wearily away," "She speaks with deliberate slowness, as though to emphasize the point," etc.) which characterizes stage directions in modern naturalistic drama. Because Greek drama is highly rhetorical and stylized, the translator knows that his words must do the real work of inflection and nuance. Therefore every effort has been made to supply the visual and tonal sense required by a given scene and the reader's (or actor's) putative unfamiliarity with the ancient conventions.

3. Numbering of lines

For the convenience of the reader who may wish to check the English against the Greek text or vice versa, the lines have been numbered according to both the Greek text and the translation. The lines of the English translation have been numbered in multiples of ten, and these numbers have been set in the right-hand margin. The (inclusive) Greek numeration will be found bracketed at the top of the page. The reader will doubtless note that in many plays the English lines out-number the Greek, but he should not therefore conclude that the translator has been unduly prolix. In most cases the reason is simply that the translator has adopted the free-flowing norms of modern Anglo-American prosody, with its brief, breath- and emphasis-determined lines, and its habit of indicating cadence and caesuras by line length and setting rather than by conventional punctuation. Other translators have preferred four-beat or five-beat lines, and in these cases Greek and English numerations will tend to converge.

4. Notes and Glossary

In addition to the Introduction, each play has been supplemented by Notes (identified by the line numbers of the translation) and a Glossary. The Notes are meant to supply information which the translators deem important to the interpretation of a passage; they also afford the translator an opportunity to justify what he has done. The Glossary is intended to spare the reader the trouble of going elsewhere to look up mythical or geographical terms. The entries are not meant to be comprehensive; when a fuller explanation is needed, it will be found in the Notes.

ABOUT THE TRANSLATION

Richmond Lattimore is indisputably the dean of American classical translators, one of the few contemporaries who belong to the great company of scholar-poets who, since the Middle Ages, have kept the classics in vigorous life. He is also one of the most prolific and versatile, ranging with easy assurance from Greek epic to lyric, tragedy, comedy, and even the Christian gospels. His corpus includes translations (many of them canonical) of the *Iliad* and the *Odyssey*, Hesiod's *Theogony*, the odes of Pindar, Greek lyric poetry, Aeschylus' *Oresteia*, Euripides' *Alcestis*, *Trojan Women*, and *Helen*, and the

Revelation of St. John. He is the author of numerous scholarly works and also a distinguished poet in his own right.

His new version of Euripides' *Iphigeneia in Tauris* exhibits all those virtues which have made his work famous. There is, first, his ability to produce a rendering which is not only remarkably faithful but also poetry of a high order. There is also his tactful and craftsmanlike humility before his original. And there is finally that elusive reticence that makes him shy away from gross or contrived effects. If the syntax seems at times under strain, the reason is the stern effort to achieve accuracy, to render the authentic feel of the Greek and give the reader the sense of reading something that is both strangely familiar and subtly remote. And this is surely as it should be. The Greek play too thoroughly domesticated into English forfeits the distance it must have in order to be assimilated on its own terms as well as ours.

Lattimore's talents, it seems to me, are peculiarly suited to *Iphigeneia in Tauris*. For this is a play which eludes definition and interpretation alike; which moves mercurially from playfulness and pathos to the powerful liberation of love of the central recognition-scene; which delicately touches tragic feelings without seriously engaging them (for it wants to transform them); and which, for all the high artistic gloss of its poetry and structure, remains a strangely moving and mysterious work, as graceful as it is reticent.

Lincoln, Vermont   William Arrowsmith

CONTENTS

IPHIGENEIA IN TAURIS

INTRODUCTION

I

Iphigeneia in Tauris was probably presented in 414 B.C. It is almost certainly later than the *Trojan Women* (415 B.C.) and earlier than *Helen* (412 B.C.). The drama in theme and structure is entirely different from the *Trojan Women* and still more strikingly similar to *Helen*. This fact has been pointed out before, but the more one studies the two plays the more similarities appear. Without claiming that the list is exhaustive, I would offer the following table:

Iphigeneia	*Helen*
The heroine has been divinely transported to the ends of the earth (the land of the Taurians on the Black Sea) and thus rescued from danger (death).	The heroine has been divinely transported to the ends of the earth (Egypt) and thus rescued from danger (abduction and rape).
The heroine opens the play by telling her story in a monologue of 66 lines.	The heroine opens the play by telling her story in a monologue of 67 lines.
The heroine is maintained in honorable captivity by the local barbarian prince, Thoas. Thoas loves Iphigeneia? Thus Goethe in his version, but, despite 1190,[1] I doubt this.	The heroine is maintained in honorable captivity by the local barbarian prince, Theoklymenos, who loves Helen and seeks to marry her.
The heroine is attended by a chorus of homesick Greek women, who are captive slaves.	The heroine is attended by a chorus of homesick Greek women, who are captive slaves.
The heroine presumes, on very slight evidence that her long-lost brother is dead, just before he appears.	The heroine presumes, on very slight evidence that her long-lost husband is dead, just before he appears.
The heroine with the Chorus mourns the death of her brother.	The heroine with the Chorus mourns the death of her husband.

1. Unless otherwise indicated, line references throughout are to my English version.

The heroine is told of the fall of Troy and the fates of various Achaians.	The heroine is told of the fall of Troy and the fates of various Achaians.
Brother and sister recognize each other.	Husband and wife recognize each other.
Brother and sister plan their escape. After two futile suggestions by the hero (one of which is the killing of the king), the heroine propounds the successful plot.	Husband and wife plan their escape. After two futile suggestions by the hero (one of which is the killing of the king), the heroine propounds the successful plot.
The escape plot uses the pretext of a religious ceremony, thus playing on the piety of the barbarian king, who grants the Greeks an escort.	The escape plot uses the pretext of a religious ceremony, thus playing on the piety of the barbarian king, who grants the Greeks an escort.
The Messenger gives the king an account of the flight in 93 lines.	The Messenger gives the king an account of the flight in 93 lines.
The king's men have suspected a trick but did not dare to act until almost too late.	The king's men have suspected a trick but did not dare to act until too late.
Pursuit is ultimately halted by a divine epiphany. The king's rage is ended and the Chorus is saved.	The escape is ultimately expounded by a divine epiphany. The king's rage is ended and his sister is saved.

In addition to these parallels, each play contains one *stasimon,* or choral ode, which has little or nothing to do with the action of the drama. These odes are divine myths, sacred stories of the gods as interludes in the adventures of heroes. In *Iphigeneia in Tauris* (1211-56) we hear of the wrath of earth against Apollo when he usurped the oracle at Delphi; in *Helen* (1301-68), of the wrath of Demeter when her daughter was ravished.

There are, of course, many noteworthy differences between the two plays. The recognition scenes, for example, are in themselves quite differently contrived. Greek plays have been shown frequently to conform, in their several portions, to certain structural conventions; that is, there are repeated forms for (especially) prologue, theophany or *deus ex machina,* messenger scene or catastrophe, dirge. These two plays, beyond other extant tragedies, conform in pattern through their entire action.

Iphigeneia in Tauris, like *Helen,* retells the *end* of a long tale of tribulation and loss, through final discovery and reunion, and points to a fortunate future for a loving pair. It is a well-made, conventional play whose author is well aware of the demands of plot. And in simple terms, it moves from bad to good rather than, like *Oedipus,* good to bad or, better, bad to worse. Such features have suggested to modern critics that our play, along with *Helen, Ion,* and many lost dramas

come va il tuo lavoro?

especially by Euripides, belongs with comedy rather than tragedy, and we hear such terms as "romantic comedy" or "tragicomedy." It is necessary to recognize that the term "tragedy" is commonly applied in modern criticism in a sense quite different from its original sense. While no critic would soberly deny that Sophocles' *Philoktetes* is a genuine tragedy, happy ending and all, we do persistently associate the term with downfall, death, disaster. Such associations have been so sanctioned by usage since the Middle Ages that they cannot be ignored. At the same time, we should realize that to call *Iphigeneia in Tauris* "not a tragedy at all" (thus Platnauer, my debt to whom is acknowledged below) would have been virtually nonsensical to Euripides, Aristotle, and Athens. The occasion and sanctions of performance, the use of heroic legend, the tragic diction and meters, the tragic actors, costumes, and every circumstance defined it as tragedy, and the happy ending made no difference. By these genuine standards, *Iphigeneia in Tauris* is just as much a tragedy as *Antigone*, just as surely as *Tosca* and *The Marriage of Figaro* are both operas.

II

nice hotels

Perhaps "romantic tragedy" is a better term (though it might remind one of *Romeo and Juliet*). I have tried elsewhere to show some essential distinctions between the happy-ending plays of Euripides and the romantic comedy of Menanader and his successors, which does in great part derive from them. But we are concerned here with the difference between *Iphigeneia in Tauris*, *Helen*, and perhaps *Ion* on the one hand, and *Medea*, *Hippolytos*, and *Herakles* on the other. For despite all the foregoing, there are vital differences, not only in story type but in dramatic quality and characterization.

What manner of dramatic person do we find in Iphigeneia, Orestes, and their lesser supporting characters? Character is expressed in action and has to do with the nature of the story. In this play, the emphasis is on what happens, and how, rather than why. Things have happened and do happen to Iphigeneia and Orestes, but their histories do not spring inevitably from anything inherent in their own natures. They are more like sets of responses than dynamic characters with insistent wills. Iphigeneia responds to events as would a good normal young woman to whom astonishing things have happened. Orestes has murdered, and is prepared to murder again if necessary, but he is not murderous; the murder is part of the whole series of events through which he has been pushed about. Brother and sister come of a house that has suffered under a curse, despite its glories, through the brilliant but bloody and corrupt saga of Pelops and Hippodameia, Atreus and Thyestes, Agamemnon and Clytemnestra. All this is recognized and alluded to, but it does not haunt the present action as in Aeschylus the present actors are haunted by a sick and sickening past. That is not the business of this play, for these people are to be the survivors escaping from adventure into respectability, which is what they desire. Iphigeneia once wanted Achilles; she will get a lifetime office attached once more to a shrine; but she will be content. The emotion is there, but it is homesickness and longing for family reunions.

Recognition and escape, action, plot, are dominant in this play. Some sacrifices are made and one can sometimes see the machinery at work. Here is an example: After the ecstasies over recognition, Pylades (880) points out that escape is now the priority. Orestes agrees. But Iphigeneia insists on extracting some further information about the family. She is entitled to know about this before we are through with her, and here is the only place the action's economy will allow it. But when the murder of Clytemnestra comes up and Iphigeneia asks about her motives, Orestes curtly cuts her off, and she meekly agrees. She is not really so meek, and shall she go through the rest of her life not knowing what Clytemnestra was about? Certainly not. But if Orestes went into that, it would not so much delay the pace of the action as alter the tone of the play, which is not about the sins of the house but about the reunion and escape of its survivors. It is very neat to make Orestes appeal to the standard of what an unmarried, still-young lady ought or ought not to be told about.

Consider also the Messenger's recounting the escape to the ship. The messenger's speech is by now a standard feature of tragedy. It gives the poet a chance to indulge his powers in straight narration— for the messenger himself is usually little more than an announcer— and was doubtless awaited with eagerness by the audience. Without it, the story of this escape would be woefully incomplete. But the messenger scene can also, sometimes, strain a too literal credulity. In Medea and Ion the Messenger begins with something like "Run for your life," and then proceeds to a deliberately detailed narrative. Here, the natural impulse of Thoas would be to rush to the scene. So he and the Messenger assure each other that escape is impossible and there is no real need for haste; and the king, and we, can listen to the story.

Such considerations may seem prosaic when applied to a beautiful poetic play; but in truth this drama is not one of the deep ones, nor is it personal, or intense. The dominant emotions are homesickness and family feeling. The Euripidean drive for escape is there, but this time it is not escape from love, sex, self, or life, but from disliked foreign climes to Greece, symbolized in the rescue of Artemis herself from her outlandish cult and her removal to civilized Attica. But the feeling of homesickness is most poignantly expressed by the captive women in the loveliest choral ode in the play (1067-1128). Behind their presence on stage one can see the Greek women from stormed cities actually sold as slaves into barbary. It is only here, through them, I think, that the time of war in which this drama was written makes itself felt. The horror of destructive war cannot be escaped in the *Trojan Women*, presented, probably, only one year earlier. In *Iphigeneia in Tauris* the women of the Chorus will, by Athena's orders, be restored to their homes. The Trojan Women, like the real women of Melos, had no homes to go to.

But our play is not, like the *Trojan Women*, an artistic expression of protest. We do not find here resentment against things as they are, or angry criticism of the gods. The gods figure mainly as manipulators. The play begins with one miracle, and ends with another; they are not miracles which Euripides, or most of his audience, was likely to believe in. Apollo has pushed Orestes here and there. When his benevolence, or competence, is challenged, this is not so much Euripides challenging divinity as a dramatic trope: the true helper thought to be false just before his truth is vindicated. Apollo seems to me to be a credible object of religious feeling only in the little amoral hymn about the baby god (1211-56). The Artemis who is a piece of consecrated wood is also an object of religious feeling, though her priestess uses her sanctity in the most cynical kind of strategy. She has to be rescued and transported by human hands with the help of another goddess; but she still retains more divinity than the story-contrivance goddess who snatched Iphigeneia away from Aulis. Iphigeneia dislikes her Taurian rites; but her criticism of illogical aspects of this cult, while standard Euripides, is aimed at human practice rather than at divinities as such. The *deus ex machina* in the conclusion facilitates the completion of the plot, and ties up most of the loose ends. It also establishes a cult, which Euripides might well have respected; and Athena, as well as being a story-goddess, represents Athens. Euripides had his complaints about Athens and his complaints about religion, but this happy-ending tragedy—and that is *not* a contradiction in terms—was not the proper medium for their expression. The gods are used here in uncontroversial terms.

III

Iphigeneia is not in Homer, unless she is the same as the Iphianassa named in Book IX of the *Iliad* (but Sophocles in his *Elektra* distinguishes them). At any rate, in Homer nobody sacrifices or attempts to sacrifice any daughter of Agamemnon. The slaughter of Iphigeneia is a constant theme in tragedy, but no extant tragedy *recounts* that slaughter. The post-Homeric epic *Kypria*[1] told how, when Iphigeneia was about to be sacrificed at Aulis, Artemis snatched her away, substituting a fawn in her place, and immortalized her among the Taurians. The rescue is also attested in a rather recently published fragment of Hesiod.[2] Hesiod calls her Iphimede, but obviously means the same heroine, since he records that the Achaians sacrificed only the image of the girl (as Paris married Helen's image only). Iphimede herself was rescued and immortalized by Artemis, like her aunt, Phylonoë, according to the same fragment. These are the earliest sources we have for Iphigeneia. On the other hand, Pindar, in his Pythian XI (either 474 or 454 B.C.), implies that Iphigeneia really was slaughtered. Aeschylus in *Agamemnon* breaks off his moving and magnificent description of the sacrifice just before the blow falls. The genuine ending of Euripides' own *Iphigeneia in Aulis* is lost; but there is evidence that in this play, too, the divine rescue took place. Sophocles, it seems, and certainly one later tragic poet had Iphigeneia survive and be found by Orestes. Thus the version in which Iphigeneia is saved is well attested, even prevalent. But all her people, as in this play, believe that she has been slaughtered; though it is difficult to reconstruct the feelings of spectators at the sacrifice at Aulis when they saw the slain fawn on the altar. Pindar and the dramatists state or suggest that her sacrifice was a motive for Clytemnestra's murder of Agamemnon. If the mother was made to believe that the sacrifice was really consummated, the poet does not have to go into the question of rescue. He can eat his cake and have it, depending on which end of the story he is telling.

This introduction began with a study of the analogies between Iphigeneia and Helen. There is one more point of resemblance. Helen was worshiped as a goddess in Sparta and Iphigeneia was immortalized and closely associated with Artemis. Herodotos in his *History* says that the goddess to whom the Taurians offered human sacrifice was, according to the Taurians themselves, Iphigeneia the daughter of

Agamemnon. Both Iphigeneia and Helen doubled as heroines and
goddesses.

IV

This translation is based on the Greek text of Gilbert Murray as published in Oxford Classical Texts, second edition, 1913. I have con-
sulted the excellent commentary of Maurice Platnauer in his edition
of the play (Oxford, 1938) at every step, and am immensely indebted.
My errors will be my own. The text as it has come down to us is full
of difficulties and corruptions. At times I have simply had to adopt a
makeshift interpretation which seemed to make some kind of sense.

Bryn Mawr, Pennslyvania   RICHMOND LATTIMORE
1972

---

1. Conveniently found in *Hesiod, the Homeric Hymns, and Homerica*, ed. H. G.
Evelyn-White, 2d ed. (Loeb Series) (London and Cambridge, Mass., 1936).

2. *Fragmenta Hesiodea*, ed. R. Merkelbach and M. L. West (Oxford, 1967).

IPHIGENEIA IN TAURIS

CHARACTERS

IPHIGENEIA daughter of Agamemnon, priestess of Artemis in the land of the
Taurians
ORESTES brother of Iphigeneia
PYLADES son of Strophios, Orestes' cousin and close friend
THOAS king of the Taurians
HERDSMAN
MESSENGER one of Thoas' guards
CHORUS of fifteen Greek women, captive slaves of Thoas
ATHENA the goddess

Girls, attendants of Iphigeneia
Guards, in charge of Orestes and Pylades
Attendants of Thoas

Line numbers in the right-hand margin of the text refer to the
English translation only, and the Notes at p. 70 are keyed to
these lines. The bracketed line numbers in the running headlines
refer to the Greek text.

Before the door of the temple of Artemis, in the Taurian country. Enter IPHIGENEIA, *alone, to speak the prologue.*

IPHIGENEIA   Pelops, the son of Tantalos, came to Pisa once
with his swift chariot, married Oinomaos' daughter,
who bore him Atreus. Atreus had sons. They were
Menelaos and Agamemnon. I am Agamemnon's child.
I am Iphigeneia, Clytemnestra's daughter.
And where Euripos strait with pulsing gusts of wind
tosses the blue sea-water and reverses it,
my father thought he sacrificed me to Artemis
because of Helen, in the famous Aulis bay.
For at that place lord Agamemnon had assembled   10
the expedition of a thousand Hellenes' ships.
He wished the crown of victory over Ilion
for the Achaians, and to avenge the marriage of Helen
outraged by violence, and to comfort Menelaos.
But hard winds were against him, and he could not sail.
He turned to divination. Kalchas said to him:
"Agamemnon, lord over this Greek armament,
you cannot clear your ship from shore till Artemis
has taken Iphigeneia, your daughter, sacrificed
by you. You vowed to offer up the loveliest thing   20
the year gave birth to, to the goddess who brings light.
Your consort Clytemnestra bore a child in your house."
(By this he meant that I was the year's loveliest gift.)
"You must offer her up." They took me from my mother
        then.
Odysseus lied, and said I was to marry Achilles.
I came to Aulis, wretched I. I was caught and held
above the death-pyre, and the sword was ready to kill.
But Artemis stole me away, and gave to the Achaians
a fawn in my place, and carried me through the bright air

13

to this land of the Taurians, and settled me here.   30
Here the lord of the country, the barbarian
Thoas, rules his barbarians. His name means swift.
He is wing-footed, and his speed makes good the name.
He has established me as priestess in this shrine.
There are rituals here; the goddess Artemis is pleased
with them: a holy service: only the name is good.
I must not tell the details, for I fear the god,
but I sacrifice, by custom known before my time
in the state, any Greek man who comes upon this shore.
I dedicate them: the real killing is left to others,   40
and done in secret in the temple of this god.
      But this past night brought with it dreams both strange
            and new.
I will tell them to the air. It may bring some relief.
I thought within my dream I had escaped this land
and lived in Argos. There I slept among my girls.
And then the earth was shaken like a stormy sea,
but I escaped and stood outside and watched the cornice
of the house fall apart, and all the covering roof
was tumbled from its high position to the ground.
One single pillar, as it seemed to me, was left   50
in my father's house, and from its capital the blond
hair streamed, and it took human voice and spoke. Then I,
faithful to my own deadly duty done to strangers,
sprinkled him with the water that prepares for death,
myself in tears. I reconstruct my vision thus.
Orestes, whom I dedicated, is now dead,
for the male children are the pillars of the house,
but those on whom my lustral waters fall must die.
I cannot make the rest of the family fit this dream.
Strophios had no children when I faced my death.   60
I wish, then, to attend the absent, give my brother
his last rites. So much I can do for him—with help
from my attendants, those Greek women given me
by the king. Where are they? For some reason or another
they have not yet arrived. I will retire to the house,
this temple of the goddess which is now my home.   *Exit*

Enter ORESTES *and* PYLADES.

ORESTES Look around. Be careful. Somebody may be on the road.

PYLADES So I do. I am looking. My eyes go everywhere.

ORESTES Pylades, do you think this is the temple
of that goddess for whom we sailed from Argos, and came
here? 70

PYLADES I think so, Orestes. You must think so too.

ORESTES And this is the altar, dripping with Hellenic blood?

PYLADES At least the top of it is brown with bloodstains.

ORESTES And hanging under the edge itself, do you see the spoils?

PYLADES Yes, skulls of slaughtered strangers, as an offering.
But it is best to take a good look all around.

ORESTES Phoibos, what trap is this? Where have you brought me now
by prophecies? I have avenged my father's blood.
I killed my mother. Relays of vindictive Furies
have driven me in flight, an exile out of my land, 80
and many are the reversing courses I have run.
I came to you and asked you how to reach the end
and respite from my headlong madness and the pain
and weariness of wandering all the length of Greece.
You told me to come here, into the Taurian land,
where Artemis, your sister, has her altar, here
to seize that image of the goddess, which they say
fell once upon this very temple from the sky.
When I have captured it, by cleverness or luck,
and won the perilous quest, I must deliver it 90
to Attic soil. Nothing was ordered beyond that.
But I shall have rest from labors when this task is done.
It was through your persuasive words that I came here

15

to this unknown unfriendly country.

                              Pylades,
You are my helper in this work. I ask for counsel.
What shall we do? You see the surrounding walls, how high
they are. Can we go straight up on the temple stair
to the door? How can we do this and remain unseen?
Can we with crowbars force apart the brazen doors?
We know of no crowbars. Furthermore, if we are caught   100
forcing the doors open, contriving entrances,
then we shall die. Sooner than die, let us escape
aboard that ship in which we made our voyage here.

PYLADES Flight is unendurable. It is not our way.
We must not spoil the force of the god's utterance.
But let us leave the temple now, and hide ourselves
in caves carved out with water by the darkening sea,
away from the ship, for fear that someone may spy the hull
and tell the king; for then we should be caught by force.
But after sunset, when the face of night comes on,   110
then we must practice all our ingenuity
and dare to steal the wooden image from the shrine.
See there between the triglyphs, there is an empty space
where one could slip inside. It is the brave who dare
adventures. Cowards never amount to anything.

ORESTES It shall not be that we have come this long sea way
and then, short of our destination, turned for home.
You are right, then, and to be obeyed. We must withdraw
and find some place in this land where we can hide
           ourselves.
The god's cause shall not be so ended that his word   120
is being spent upon futility. We must be bold,
for hardship offers no excuse when men are young.

                Exeunt. Enter the CHORUS *and* IPHIGENEIA

CHORUS Silence, oh silence,
all who dwell by the Clashing Rocks

on the unfriendly sea.
Daughter of Leto,
Diktynna of the wild mountains,
to your court, to the golden
wall of the columned temple,
I come with devout and maidenly step,   130
slave to the devout key-bearer,
exiled from the walls and towers of Greece,
from forest range and grassland,
exiled from Europe
and the mansion house of my fathers.
I am here. What is new? What care is yours,
O daughter of Agamemnon
who came against the fortress of Troy
with his famous fleet,
the thousand ships   140
and thousands and thousands of armed men?

IPHIGENEIA O my attendant women,
hard mourning melodies are my task,
discordant singing of sorrows,
lyreless complaints
the tears of pity.
Disaster has fallen upon me.
I mourn the death of my brother.
Such was the vision I saw,
a dream in my sleep   150
in the dark of the night now ended.
Ruin, I am ruined.
The house of my father is gone;
its seed is perished.
Alas, the sorrows of Argos.
O divine spirit,
you robbed me of my sole brother, sent him
to Hades; for him I prepare
the bowl of libations poured for the perished
to splash on earth's surface: 160
streams of milk from the mountain cattle,

wine, the liquid of Bacchus,
the artful work of the tawny bees:
charms for the dead established by use.

Give me the all-gold vessel
and the libations for Hades.

O scion of Agamemnon, beneath
the ground, I give you this, as to one dead.
Accept. I shall not bring my tears
nor my blond hair to your tomb.   170
I have been exiled far from the land
which is yours and mine, and where I am thought
to have been killed, to lie buried.

CHORUS I will sing you an answering song,
the Asian strain, the barbarian dirge,
mistress, the melody used
in lamentation,
dirges for the dead, the song that is sung
by Hades, no peal of triumph.
Alas for the house of Atreus and his line.   180
The light of their scepters is gone
from the house of your fathers.
There was a reign of prospering kings
in Argos once
and trouble on trouble assailed them.
There was the charioteer hurled out
by Pelops once from his flying chariot,
and the sacred gleam of the sun forsook
his former place. A succession of pains
befell the house because of the golden lamb,   190
murder on murder, grief on grief.
Thus for those of the Tantalid line
who were killed before, retribution comes
on the house, and the spirit inflicts on you
what should not be.

To mourn Orestes

IPHIGENEIA My fortune has been misfortune
since the bridal night of my mother
when I was conceived; from the outset
the divine fates who were present
at my birth have schooled me in hardship.   200
My mother, sad daughter of Leda,
was courted among the Hellenes.
I was her first child born in her chambers.
For sacrifice and for slaughter
unhallowed, for the disgrace of my father
she bore and raised me.
In a chariot drawn by horses
they brought me to the sands of Aulis,
a bride cursed in her bridal
for Achilles, son of the Nereid.   210
Now, an alien by the unfriendly sea,
without marriage or child, without city or friend,
I am housed in an arid country.
I do not dance for Argive Hera,
nor on the murmuring loom
work out with my shuttle the pictured form
of Titans and Pallas Athena;
but with bloody and harsh music
I work bloody despair of strangers
whose cries are pitiful   220
as are pitiful the tears they shed.
But now I forget my pity for these,
and bewail the dead man in Argos,
my brother, whom I left as a child at the breast,
still a baby, growing and flourishing,
in his mother's arms, held fast to her breast,
and prince of Argos, Orestes.

CHORUS I see a herdsman coming in our direction.
He comes from the sea shore, with something to report.

Enter the HERDSMAN

19

Inconsistency

HERDSMAN Daughter of Agamemnon and of Clytemnestra   230
I bring you news of strange happenings. Hear my story.

IPHIGENEIA What is startling about the story you have to tell?

HERDSMAN Two young men have slipped through the dark and clashing
                rocks
in their ship, and made their way to our country. They will be
a sacrifice and a burnt offering that will please
the goddess Artemis. Make ready then the water
and other preparations. You cannot act too soon.

IPHIGENEIA Where are they from? What country's costume do they
                wear?

HERDSMAN They are Greeks, but that is all I know about them.

IPHIGENEIA You did not hear either of the strangers use a name?   240

HERDSMAN I heard one of them call the other Pylades.

IPHIGENEIA What then was the name of this stranger's companion?

HERDSMAN Nobody knows that. We heard nothing.

IPHIGENEIA How did you happen to see them and to capture them?

HERDSMAN By the sea side, at the beach of the unfriendly strait . . .

IPHIGENEIA (*interrupting*) What have oxherds to do with the sea?

HERDSMAN We had gone down to bathe our cattle in the water.

IPHIGENEIA Come back to my first question, how you captured them
and by what means, since this is what I wish to hear.
They have been long in coming. Never yet has blood   250
of Greeks been shed upon the altar of the goddess.

20

HERDSMAN When we had brought our forest-feeding cattle down
　　　　　into the sea that flows between the Clashing Rocks,
　　　　　there was a cave in the cliffs that had been hollowed
　　　　　by the breaking of much surf, where purple-fishers camp.
　　　　　In there one herdsman of our company espied
　　　　　a pair of young men. He came back to us again
　　　　　walking on tiptoe very carefully, and said:
　　　　　"There are some gods sitting in there. Will you not go
　　　　　and look?" One of our number then, a pious man,　　　　260
　　　　　looked in the cave, then raised his arms in the air and
　　　　　　　　prayed:
　　　　　"Son of Leukothea of the sea, savior of ships,
　　　　　Palaimon, lord, be gracious, and be gracious too
　　　　　if you are the Dioscuri who are seated there,
　　　　　nurslings dear to Nereus, who is the father
　　　　　of Nereids, all fifty in their lovely choir."
　　　　　But there was another, a rough man, lawless and rude,
　　　　　who laughed at prayers, said they were shipwrecked
　　　　　　　　mariners
　　　　　who had taken refuge in the cave, fearing our custom,
　　　　　having been told of how we sacrifice outlanders.　　　　270
　　　　　This man was right, most of us thought, and we resolved
　　　　　to seize and offer them to the god, as is our rule.

　　　　　　　　Meanwhile, one of the strangers came out of the cave
　　　　　and stood there, shaking his head up and down, trembling
　　　　　to the fingertips, and screamed aloud, caught in some fit
　　　　　of madness, and cried out, the way a hunter cries:
　　　　　"Pylades, there, did you see her? There's another one,
　　　　　a serpent of the god of death, who tries to kill me,
　　　　　and arms against me all the vipers of her hair.
　　　　　Another, blasting fire and murder from her clothes,　　　280
　　　　　swoops over me on beating wings. She holds my mother
　　　　　in her arms, to drop her on me like a weight of stone.
　　　　　Oh, she will kill me. Where shall I run?" There was nothing
　　　　　　　　there
　　　　　to be seen that looked like any such creatures. He mistook
　　　　　the voices of the lowing cattle and barking dogs,
　　　　　and thought they reproduced the clamor of the Furies.

21

We drew together in a group, and held our place,
silent and wondering; but then he drew his sword
and like a lion sprang into the midst of the cows
and laid about him with the steel, struck flank and rib,   290
thinking so to beat off the divine Furies' attack.
He made the surface of the sea bloom bright with blood.
At this, all of us, when we saw our pastured herds
were being felled, wasted and ruined, rushed to arms
and blew the sea-horns to arouse the neighborhood.
We thought that we, mere herdsmen, were too weak to fight
these foreign men who were so young and strongly built.
We grew into a multitude, though it took time.
Now the young man, after his fit was gone, fell down
with the foam running down his chin. We, seeing him   300
felled and at our mercy, then did all we could
to stone and pelt him, but the other foreigner
wiped the foam from his face, guarded the prostrate man,
and held his handsome woven robe in front of him,
dodging the dangerous missiles that we threw at both
and doing everything he could to help his friend.
And now, restored to sanity, the fallen man
sprang up, and saw the tide of war that threatened them
and the advancing ruin that was all but there.
He groaned; but we did not give up our shower of stones   310
and kept attacking, now from this side, now from that,
until we heard the dread cry of encouragement:
"Pylades, we must die, but if we must die then
with all honor. Out with your sword and follow me."
We, when we saw the onset of two waving swords,
ran back, and filled the stony gullies with our numbers,
but where some fled, others would then attack in turn
and throw at them; then if they turned and stabbed at these,
those who had run away before would now throw stones.
But it was unbelievable. So many threw,   320
but none could hit the destined victims of the god.
At last we beat them, not by courage or by strength,
but we surrounded them and with a shower of stones

knocked the swords from their hands, and they, for sheer
      fatigue,
sank to the ground. So we conveyed them to the king
of the country. He looked at them and sent them to you
with all speed, for consecration and for sacrifice.
Young mistress, you were praying that such foreigners
be yours to offer up. If you can waste this kind of stranger
in numbers, Hellas thus shall give you satisfaction   330
for their attempt to murder you in Aulis once.

CHORUS This was a strange tale of the mad man, who lived once
in Hellas, and has come to our unfriendly sea.

IPHIGENEIA Very well. Go fetch the strangers then, and bring them to
      me.
I shall see to the sacraments that take place here.
O wretched heart of mine, you were considerate
toward strangers formerly, and always pitied them.
The tie of kinship could be measured by your tears
whenever it was Greeks who came into your hands.
But now, by reason of my dream, which has made me fierce   340
because I think Orestes sees daylight no more,
you who arrive from this time forth will find me harsh.
For here, friends, is a truth which I have just now learned.
When people are unfortunate, their suffering
makes them no kinder to those even less fortunate.
But no wind sent from Zeus has ever come to us,
nor any vessel through the Clashing Rocks, that brought
me Helen, the one who ruined me, nor Menelaos.
Had they been in my power, I could have punished them,
making this place an Aulis like that other Aulis   350
where, like a young calf, I was seized by the Danaans
as a victim, and the sacrificer was my father.
I never can forget the sorrows of that time,
how many times I tried to clutch my father's chin
or throw my arms around his knees and cling to them.
Thus I would babble: "Father, this is my marriage time,

but you have made it into a thing of shame. While you
are killing me, my mother and the Argive women
are singing marriage songs, and all the house is full
of flute music, while I am being killed by you.   360
Achilles is then no son of Peleus. He is Death.
I am his bride. You tempted, and escorted me
treacherously by chariot to a bloody marriage."
I had kept my face and eyes behind my delicate veil.
I could not bring myself to throw my arms around
my brother, who is dead now, nor to kiss the lips
of my sister. I was bashful, being on the way
to Peleus' house, but I was saving many kisses
for the time when I would visit Argos once again.
Now, poor Orestes, if you are dead, from what high hopes   370
your father had and from what splendors are you fallen.

　　　But the goddess is too subtle. I do not approve.
When she considers any mortal stained with blood,
if only from childbirth or from contact with a corpse,
she keeps him from her altars, thinking him unclean,
while she herself is pleased with human sacrifice.
It is impossible that Leto, bride of Zeus,
produced so unfeeling a child. I myself think
the tale of how Tantalos entertained the gods
by feeding them his son, is not to be believed.   380
I also think these people, being murderous,
put off the blame for their own vice upon the gods.
I do not think any divinity is bad.

CHORUS　Dark oh dark
　　　meeting-place of two seas
　　　where Io driven and flying came
　　　from Argos to the Euxine
　　　and made the change
　　　from Europe over to Asia.
　　　But who are these? Was it from the reedy sweet stream   390
　　　of Eurotas they left behind
　　　or the hallowed waters of Dirke
　　　when they came to this inhospitable land

where the altars and porticoed
temple of the bright maiden
are stained with the blood of humans?

Or did they sail
with double beat of the fir-wood
oars across the surge of the sea,
riding with sails wind-driven   400
upon a distant quest
to increase their halls' treasures?
For hope is fond, and, to people's misfortune,
insatiable for the persons
who bring back the rich cargoes,
wanderers over the sea to the cities and the outlanders.
All with one single
purpose; sometimes their judgment of profit
fails; sometimes it attains.

How did they pass the Clashing Rocks,   410
how pass the sleepless strands
of Phineus' harpies,
running across
the foam to the far beach
of Amphitrite,
where the chorus of fifty girls,
the Nereids, step and weave their dance
circles? How did they pass
as the cradled oars
sang at the stern before airs   420
that filled the sail,
blowing from the south
or winds from the west
to the land where the birds gather,
the white strand where Achilles
runs his shining races
along the unfriendly sea?

If only my mistress' prayers

could come true, and Helen,
Leda's darling daughter,   430
could come here
on her way from Troy, and with deadly
lustral water poured on her hair
die with her throat cut
by the hand of our mistress,
and pay the penalty she deserves.
/// But the sweetest news I could hear
would be that some seafarer
from Greece had arrived
to put an end to the pain   440
of my sad slavery.
/// For in my dreams I would be
in my house and my father's city,
to enjoy the delight of our songs,
a grace shared by all of us.

ORESTES *and* PYLADES *are brought in by temple attendants.*

But here, with their hands bound, leaning
on each other, are the two young men, a fresh
sacrifice to the goddess. Hush, dear friends,
for these are a choice offering
from Greece who come to our temple.   450
The oxherd man
told us, then, no false story.
/// Goddess, if you are pleased with the way
of this city, accept the sacrifice;
but our custom in Greece
declares that it is not holy.

IPHIGENEIA So.
My first consideration must be for the goddess
and how to please her. Now untie the strangers' hands.
They are sacred victims and must be no longer bound.   460
Go into the temple and have everything in order
which is needed and customary for our present business.

26

Attendants go into the temple. IPHIGENEIA *contemplates*
ORESTES *and* PYLADES

Who was the mother who gave you birth? Who was your
    father?
Who is your sister? Did you ever have a sister?
What a pair of young brothers she has lost in you
and will be brotherless. Who knows which ones will suffer
this kind of loss? The progress of the gods' designs
goes through the dark. Our own misfortunes are unknown.
Fortune twists everything, so it is hard to see.

Where do you come from, O unhappy travelers?   470
You have sailed a great distance in order to reach this land,
and, far from home, must spend eternity below.

ORESTES Why, mistress, whoever you are, these words of pity,
    thus adding to the pain we must look forward to?
    I find no wisdom in one who, about to kill,
    tries to combat the fear of death by sympathy,
    nor one who comforts a person on the brink of death
    but gives no hope of rescue. Out of a single evil
    he makes two, by being silly, while the victim
    dies anyway. We should take fortune as it comes.   480
    Stop being sorry for us. We well understand
    the kind of sacrifice that is conducted here.

IPHIGENEIA Which of you two is the one who was addressed by name
    as Pylades? This is the first thing I would know.

ORESTES He is. Do you get any pleasure from learning that?

IPHIGENEIA Of which city in Greece is he a citizen?

ORESTES What good would it do you, mistress, if we told you that?

IPHIGENEIA Are you brothers, then, born of a single mother?

ORESTES Brothers in love we are, but not brothers by birth.

IPHIGENEIA What was the name that your father bestowed on you?   490

ORESTES The right name to call me would be Unlucky Man.

IPHIGENEIA That is not what I mean. Give that name to your fate.

ORESTES If we die nameless, no one can insult our names.

IPHIGENEIA But why do you begrudge me? Are you then so proud?

ORESTES It will be my body, not my name, you sacrifice.

IPHIGENEIA Will you not even tell me what your city is?

ORESTES It will do no good to answer. I am going to die.

IPHIGENEIA But what prevents you from doing me this favor?

ORESTES I claim glorious Argos for my fatherland.

IPHIGENEIA In the gods' name, is that true, my friend? Were you born
          there?   500

ORESTES I am from Mycenae, which was once a prospering city.

IPHIGENEIA Are you an exile from your land, or what has happened?

ORESTES I am an involuntary voluntary exile.

IPHIGENEIA Now will you tell me one more thing I wish to know?

ORESTES I suppose so. My misfortune gives me plenty of time.

IPHIGENEIA But your arrival from Argos is a welcome thing.

ORESTES I do not welcome it, but you may, if you like.

IPHIGENEIA Perhaps you know of Troy, which is spoken of everywhere.

ORESTES I wish I had never even dreamed of its existence.

IPHIGENEIA They say the spear has captured it and the town is gone.   510

ORESTES That is the truth, and what they told you was accurate.

IPHIGENEIA Has Helen come back to the house of Menelaos?

ORESTES She has. It was bad news for one of my family.

IPHIGENEIA Where is she? I also owe her no good will.

ORESTES She is in Sparta, living with her former husband.

IPHIGENEIA Hateful to all the Greeks and not to me alone.

ORESTES I too have been affected because she ran away.

IPHIGENEIA Did the Achaians reach home, as the rumor goes?

ORESTES You are asking me to tell you everything at once.

IPHIGENEIA Before you die, I would like to hear everything.   520

ORESTES Ask then, since that is what you want, and I will answer.

IPHIGENEIA Did a certain prophet called Kalchas ever come back from
      Troy?

ORESTES The report in Mycenae was that he is dead.

IPHIGENEIA Thanks to be Artemis. What of Odysseus, Laertes' son?

ORESTES The story was that he was alive, but not returned.

IPHIGENEIA A curse on him. I hope he dies and never comes home.

ORESTES Curse him no more. His fortunes are in a sorry state.

IPHIGENEIA Achilles, son of Nereid Thetis—is he alive?

ORESTES No. His marriage at Aulis was an empty thing.

IPHIGENEIA It was betrayal. Those who suffered from it know.   530

ORESTES Who are you? You ask so knowingly about Greece.

IPHIGENEIA I am from there. I was lost when still a child.

ORESTES Naturally, then, you wish to know what happened there.

IPHIGENEIA What of the general whom they call "the fortunate man?"

ORESTES Who? The general I am thinking of was not fortunate.

IPHIGENEIA There was one called Agamemnon, son of Atreus.

ORESTES I do not know, mistress. Please leave that subject alone.

IPHIGENEIA I implore you by the gods, tell me, just to please me.

ORESTES The unhappy man is dead. His death ruined another.

IPHIGENEIA Dead? How could that have happened? How I grieve for
             him.   540

ORESTES Why this lament? Was he somehow related to you?

IPHIGENEIA I grieve over his former great prosperity.

ORESTES He died in a terrible fashion, murdered by his wife.

IPHIGENEIA I weep for her, who killed him, and for him, who died.

ORESTES Stop now, and do not ask me any more about it.

IPHIGENEIA Only this: is the murdered man's wife living still?

ORESTES She is not; and her murderer is her own son.

IPHIGENEIA The house is all in ruins. How could he do it? Why?

ORESTES To take revenge upon her for his father's death.

IPHIGENEIA Ah.   550
How just, how evil was this righteous punishment.

ORESTES Though he is just, he gets no favor from the gods.

IPHIGENEIA Are other children of Agamemnon still in the house?

ORESTES He left one daughter, Elektra, a girl still young.

IPHIGENEIA What do you hear of the daughter who was sacrificed?

ORESTES Only that she is dead and sees the light no more.

IPHIGENEIA She suffered much. Her father, who killed her, suffered too.

ORESTES Her death was a graceless grace for a bad woman's sake.

IPHIGENEIA The son of that man killed in Argos—does he live?

ORESTES He lives, a wretched man, nowhere and everywhere.   560

IPHIGENEIA False dreams, farewell; you never meant anything after all.

ORESTES Nor are the gods, who are considered wise by men,
any more to be trusted than the flying dreams.
There is much confusion in the workings of the gods
as there is among mortals: only one thing hurts,
when one who has good sense has listened to the words
of prophets and is ruined, as the wise men know.

31

CHORUS   Alas, but what of us then and our own parents?
         Are they alive or not? Who will ever tell us?

IPHIGENEIA   Listen to me, for I have come upon a plan   570
         which will be to your advantage, friends, but also help
         my cause. All enterprises have the most success
         when all who are involved have common interest.
         If I could save you, would you be willing to take a message
         to Argos and deliver it to my family there:
         a letter, that is, which a prisoner wrote for me?
         He was sorry for me, and he did not think my hand
         was murderous, but knew that victims of the goddess
         must die, because the goddess holds that custom good.
         I had no messenger who could go back for me   580
         to Argos and, if he survived, carry my letter,
         and deliver it to someone in my family there.
         You, therefore—if, as it now seems you do not hate me,
         and since you know Mycenae, and those whom I want—
         save your own life, with a reward that is not mean.
         Be rescued just for carrying a little note.
                 But this man, since the state enforces it, must be
         kept back and sacrificed to the divinity.

ORESTES   All you have said was good, mistress, except one thing.
         His sacrifice would be a burden on my soul.   590
         I am the man in charge of this shipload of grief;
         he sails along out of sympathy for my troubles.
         Thus, to do you a favor and myself escape
         from danger is unfair, if it costs him his life.
         Let it be done this way. Give the tablet to him.
         He will take it to Argos, so you will be satisfied.
         Let anyone, who wants to, kill me. It is shameful
         when a man drops his friendship because times are bad
         and saves himself. This man is truly dear to me.
         I value his life no less than I do my own.   600

IPHIGENEIA   O brave spirit! You must be born of noble stock,
         and are a true friend to your friends. Oh, how I hope

that the one male survivor of my family
is such as you are. Yes, friends, since I also am not
without a brother—only that I never see him.
Since you so wish it, we shall send the other man
to take the letter for me, while you die. It seems
evident that his safety is your great concern.

ORESTES Who will endure the horror of sacrificing me?

IPHIGENEIA I. For this goddess, this is my service to perform.   610

ORESTES A grim and thankless office for a girl to have.

IPHIGENEIA I am constrained to do it, and must keep the law.

ORESTES You are a woman. Can you kill men with a sword?

IPHIGENEIA No. I will sprinkle lustral water on your hair.

ORESTES Who is the slaughterer, if I may ask that question?

IPHIGENEIA There are people in the temple who attend to this.

ORESTES And what shall be my burial, when I am dead?

IPHIGENEIA A sacred fire inside, and a great cleft in the rock.

ORESTES Oh, how I wish my sister's hand could tend my body.

IPHIGENEIA Poor man, whoever you may be, that was a vain wish,   620
since she is settled far from any barbaric shore.
But still, since it is true that you are Argive born,
I shall omit no grace that I can give to you.
I shall lay many ornaments upon your bier,
and make your body soft with yellow olive oil,
and cast upon your pyre the flower-fragrant pride
of honey that the brown bee makes among the hills.
But I go now to fetch the tablet from the shrine

of the goddess. Only do not hate me for my duty.
Guard them, attendants. Do not use the manacles.   630
Perhaps I shall give that one whom I love the most
of my loved ones in Argos news beyond his hopes;
this letter, telling him that those thought dead are still
alive, will give the glad news, and he will believe.

CHORUS I grieve for you, devoted
to this bloody lustral spray.

ORESTES No cause for grief, friends; but I thank you for the thought.

CHORUS (*to* PYLADES) We are happy in your blest fortune,
young man, that you yet will tread
the soil of your native land.   640

PYLADES Friends would not want this, if it means that friends must
die.

CHORUS Oh, the errand is grim.
You also are brought to grief.
Which lot of the two is worse?
My heart still hesitates over the doubtful choice
to mourn you, who must die, or you, who must survive.

ORESTES Pylades, in God's name, are you struck by what strikes me?

PYLADES I do not know. You ask me what I cannot answer.

ORESTES Who is this girl? How like a very Greek she spoke
and questioned us about the wars at Ilion,   650
the homecoming of the Achaians, Kalchas skilled
in augury, and named Achilles, how she sorrowed
over unhappy Agamemnon, questioned me
about his wife and children. Yes, this stranger is
Argive by birth, from there. She would not otherwise
be sending a letter there, would not have questioned me
as if the Argive fortune were her fortune too.

34

PYLADES You are a little beyond me, and I would agree
with what you said first, except for one thing: all men know
the sorrows of kings, when they have had to do with them.   660
But I was going in my mind over something else.

ORESTES What is it? Share it with me. Thus you can think better.

PYLADES I would be shamed to see the daylight while you die.
I shared your voyage. I must also share your death.
I shall be established as a weakling and a coward
in Argos, also in the Phocians' land of valleys.
The multitude—the multitude is bad—will think
that I betrayed you to come home alone alive,
or even killed you, seeing the weakness of your house,
and devised murder for the sake of your kingly power,   670
being wed to your sister, who holds the inheritance.
All this I fear and hold shameful; it cannot be
otherwise; I must draw my last breath when you do,
be sacrificed with you and have my body burned
because I feared reproach and proved I was your friend.

ORESTES Hush. Speak no blasphemy. I must bear my own troubles,
but still not bear them double when they could be single.
All that which you call painful, and which will bring
              reproach,
remains for me, if I kill you after you shared
my sufferings. It is not really bad for me   680
to end my life, since the gods make it what it is.
You are a happy man, you hold a house that's clean,
not sick, like mine; my house is cursed and evil-starred.
If you survive, and beget children from my sister
whom I have given you to have and hold as wife,
our name might be continued, and my father's house
not be obliterated with no children born.
Go on your way, and live, and hold your father's house.
But when you come to Hellas and horse-breeding Argos,
I lay this charge upon you. Give me your right hand.   690
Heap up a burial mound and monument to me,

35

and let my sister give the grave her tears and hair.
Announce that I have perished by the hand of a woman
from Argos, dedicated to the altar of death.
Never forsake my sister, just because you see
that you are marrying into a family with no head.
Goodbye. You are the dearest friend that I have found,
my fellow huntsman, raised to manhood at my side,
who bore with me the many burdens of my grief.
      Phoibos is a diviner, but he lied to me.   700
He applied his arts and drove me to the farthest point
from Greece, for shame over the prophecies he spoke.
I gave him everything I had, followed his word
and killed my mother. Now I am myself destroyed.

PYLADES Your grave shall be given you, and I will not betray
your sister's bed, unhappy friend, since you must be
my friend among the dead, not one who sees the light.
But the god's prophecy to you has not yet come
to nothing, even though you stand so close to death.
Still it is true, it is, that extreme suffering   710
provides extreme reversals, when the luck is changed.

ORESTES No more! The words of Phoibos are no use to me.
Here is the lady; she is coming from the temple.

IPHIGENEIA (to the attendants) Withdraw, all of you. Go to those who
             are entrusted
with the sacrificing, and make ready all within.
(To ORESTES and PYLADES) Here is the letter-tablet with its
             many folds,
my friends. But there is something more I wish to say.
Hear me. A man is not the same man in distress
and when, with fear past, he is once more confident.
I am afraid that he who is to take the letter   720
to Argos, once he finds himself in his own land,
may never think again about my messages.

ORESTES What do you wish, then? What do you find difficult?

IPHIGENEIA He must give me an oath that he will carry this letter
to Argos, and take it to my loved ones, as I wish.

ORESTES Then will you give him in return the self-same oath?

IPHIGENEIA Yes, tell me. What must I not do? What must I do?

ORESTES Release him free and living from this barbarous land.

IPHIGENEIA Fair enough. How else could he be my messenger?

ORESTES Yes, but will the lord of the land agree to that?   730

IPHIGENEIA He will. I will persuade him
and I myself will see your friend aboard his ship.

ORESTES (*to* PYLADES) Swear, Pylades. (*To* IPHIGENEIA) Dictate the
oath religion asks.

IPHIGENEIA Then he must say: "I will give this to those you love."

PYLADES I will duly present this note to those you love.

IPHIGENEIA And I will get you safely away past the Black Rocks.

PYLADES Which of the gods do you name as witness to your oath?

IPHIGENEIA Artemis, in whose temple I officiate.

PYLADES And I invoke the lord of the sky, Zeus the august.

IPHIGENEIA What would you suffer, if you wrong me and fail your oath?   740

PYLADES Never reach home. And you, if you do not rescue me?

IPHIGENEIA Never set foot on Argos as long as I live.

PYLADES But note this other point, which we have overpassed.

IPHIGENEIA We shall make some addition, if the point is good.

PYLADES Then grant me this exception, if the ship goes down,
and if this letter, with the cargo, disappears
into the sea, and I can only save myself,
that this oath will no longer be binding on me.

IPHIGENEIA Here's what I will do. There are many possibilities.
I will inform you verbally of the whole message   750
contained and written down inside the folded tablet.
That is secure. If you can carry the letter through,
the silent writing then will tell its own message;
but if the written letter is lost in the sea,
you will save my message, if you only save yourself.

PYLADES That was well said, both for your own sake and for mine.
Name me the person in Argos to whom I should give
this letter, and the message I should repeat from you.

IPHIGENEIA Then say this to Orestes, Agamemnon's son:
"Iphigeneia, sacrificed at Aulis, sends   760
this message. She is alive, although thought dead at home."

ORESTES Where is she? Did she die? Did she come back to life?

IPHIGENEIA I am Iphigeneia. Do not break my thread.
"Bring me to Argos, O my brother, before I die.
Release me from barbarian country and the god's
sacrifices, in which my rites mean strangers' deaths."

ORESTES Pylades, what shall I say? Where do we find ourselves?

IPHIGENEIA "Or I shall be a spirit who will haunt your house,
Orestes." I repeat the name, so you will know it.

PYLADES O gods.   770

IPHIGENEIA Why do you summon the gods? This case is mine.

PYLADES   No matter. Continue. I was thinking of something else.
          Presently I will return to the question of these marvels.

IPHIGENEIA   Tell him that I was saved by the goddess Artemis
          who substituted the fawn my father sacrificed,
          supposing that with the sharp sword he struck me home.
          She settled me in this country. Those are your instructions.
          This is the message written in the closed tablets.

PYLADES   How easy are the oaths that you have bound me in
          and sworn me to most fairly. I will not wait long,   780
          but I shall validate the oath I swore to you.
                    Behold, Orestes! I deliver here to you
          the letter that was given me by your sister's hand.

ORESTES   And I accept, but will postpone reading the letter
          to seize a joy expressed in action, not in words.
          Oh, dearest sister, though astonished, I will still
          embrace you in these arms that scarcely dare believe,
          and, told of wonders, rush to take delight with you.

                    He attempts to embrace IPHIGENEIA, *who resists him.*

CHORUS   Sir, you do wrong! This is the priestess of the god
          whose clothing, never to be defiled, your arms profane.   790

ORESTES   O sister, my own sister from a single sire,
          daughter of Agamemnon, do not turn from me.
          You have me here, your brother, as you never hoped.

IPHIGENEIA   I have you for my brother? Stop it, will you not?
          Argos contains him now and Nauplia is his place.

ORESTES   O cruel one, your brother is not in those parts.

IPHIGENEIA   The Spartan, daughter of Tyndareos, gave you birth?

ORESTES   To Agamemnon, Pelops' grandson. I am his.

IPHIGENEIA Tell me then, do you have some evidence of this?

ORESTES I do. Ask me some question about my father's house.   800

IPHIGENEIA Rather, you should speak first and I shall be the judge.

ORESTES Very well. Here first is something that Elektra told.
You know the rivalry of Atreus and Thyestes?

IPHIGENEIA I have heard. There was a quarrel over the golden lamb.

ORESTES You know you wove a pretty pattern of the scene?

IPHIGENEIA Oh, good! You reach very close to my memory.

ORESTES It had an image of the sun changing its course?

IPHIGENEIA I wove that picture also with my dainty threads.

ORESTES Your mother gave you lustral water, to take to Aulis?

IPHIGENEIA I remember. No happy marriage has made me forget.   810

ORESTES What then? Did you cut your hair and give it to your
mother?

IPHIGENEIA My cenotaph, for memory of my lost body.

ORESTES Now I will give you evidence of what I saw:
the ancient spear of Pelops in our father's house.
Wielding it in his hands he killed Oinomaos,
and won Hippodameia, the Pisatid girl.
This was hidden away in your own maiden room.

IPHIGENEIA (embracing him) O dearest, dearest. That is my only name
for you.
I hold you now, grown to manhood as you are,
but far from Argos, my dear.   820

40

ORESTES   And I hold you, the one who was thought dead.
          Tears, in mourning and joy combined,
          drench your eyes and mine.

IPHIGENEIA This is the child
          I left still in his nurse's arms,
          a baby still in the house.
          Oh, happiness greater than words can tell,
          my soul, what shall I say?
          This passes wonder and speech.

ORESTES   I hope our life together still will be so good.   830

IPHIGENEIA A strange thing, friends, the joy I have won.
          I fear he might slip away out of my hands
          winging into the air.
          O Cyclopean hearth, beloved
          Mycenae, my country,
          I thank you for his life, I thank you for his nurture,
          because you raised this brother
          to light our house.

ORESTES   We are fortunate in our birth, my sister, but our life
          has been unhappy, with disasters in its course.   840

IPHIGENEIA I know it, wretched I, I remember
          my harsh father's knife against my throat.

ORESTES   Oh, I can see you, though I was not even there.

IPHIGENEIA Never a bride, my brother, to Achilles,
          when I was led to his shelter and that
          false promise of marriage.
          Beside the altar there were tears and wailing for me.
          The lustral water was there.

ORESTES   I too groan because our father was so hard-hearted.

IPHIGENEIA The father I was given was no father,   850
            and suffering follows suffering still.
            Some divinity sends it.

ORESTES But if, O wretched one, you had killed your brother?

IPHIGENEIA Oh terrible, terrible that daring
            I had then, my brother; by so little
            did you escape an impious death at my hands
            which would have torn you.
            But now, what will be the end of it all?
            What chance will come my way?
            What route can I find   860
            to send you away from the city, away from slaughter
            back to your Argive home
            before the sword draws your blood?
            O hard-pressed soul, this is your task,
            to find some means.
            Shall it be by land, not by ship?
            But, trusting to flying feet,
            you will find your death, going through barbarous tribes
            and roads that are no roads; but through the narrow strait
            by the black rock is a far way   870
            for sea-borne escape.
            Wretched, wretched am I.
            What god or mortal man
            or creature of mystery
            can find an impossible way
            for the two last children of Atreus
            to escape from evil?

CHORUS As witness, not from hearsay, I will testify
        to these events, marvels and past the power of words.

PYLADES When those beloved come into the presence of those they
                    love,   880
         Orestes, it is proper to embrace; but now
         you must leave commiserations and return to facts,

42

so we may seize on safety, gloriously named,
and take ourselves away from this barbarian land.
For prudent men, when they are not yet free from fortune,
seize further joys by seizing opportunity.

ORESTES Well said; and yet I think that fortune has in mind
to help us in this matter; yet when one is keen,
divinity can be expected to gain strength.

IPHIGENEIA You must not keep me from my question, nor prevent   890
my asking you about Elektra, and what fate
is hers, since you and she are all I have to love.

ORESTES (indicating PYLADES) With this man she enjoys a happy
married life.

IPHIGENEIA Where then does this man come from, and whose son is he?

ORESTES His father is the famous Strophios of Phocis.

IPHIGENEIA He is son of Atreus' daughter, and a relative?

ORESTES He is our cousin, and he is my one true friend.

IPHIGENEIA He was not born yet, when our father sought to kill me.

ORESTES He was not born. Strophios was childless a long time.

IPHIGENEIA I give you greeting, Pylades, husband of my sister.   900

ORESTES He is not only my kinsman, but my rescuer.

IPHIGENEIA How could you dare that awful thing done to our mother?

ORESTES To avenge my father; let us speak of it no more.

IPHIGENEIA But what reason did she have for killing her husband?

ORESTES Let my mother be; it is not proper for you to hear.

IPHIGENEIA I obey. Does Argos look to you for leadership?

ORESTES To Menelaos. I am exiled from my country.

IPHIGENEIA But could our uncle so outrage our weakened house?

ORESTES Not he. The Furies' terror drove me from the land.

IPHIGENEIA This was the seizure they reported from the beach?   910

ORESTES My wretchedness was seen, and not for the first time.

IPHIGENEIA I understand; they harry you, for our mother's sake.

ORESTES The bit is bloody that they force into my mouth.

IPHIGENEIA Why have you had to cross the sea and walk this shore?

ORESTES Prophetic orders from Apollo made me come.

IPHIGENEIA Why? Can you tell me, or is it a holy secret?

ORESTES I can tell you. Here is how my many toils began.
After my quarrel with my mother forced my act—
I will not speak of that—the onslaught of the Furies
drove me in flight, until Apollo Loxias   920
guided my feet to Athens, so as there to give
due satisfaction to the nameless goddesses.
A sacred judgment takes place there, which Zeus ordained
for Ares, when his hands were stained with guilty blood.
When I came there, nobody in the city
would take me in; they thought the gods all hated me.
Then some took pity on me. These arranged for me
a table to myself, though they were in the house,
and their silence made me one unspoken to

so I should be no part of their feast, nor of their drinking.   930
They filled an individual vessel for each man
with equal stints of wine, and so enjoyed themselves.
Since I did not presume to argue with my hosts,
I suffered in silence and pretended not to notice,
while mourning that I was my mother's murderer.
I hear that the Athenians have based a custom
on my misfortunes, and the usage still obtains
with Pallas' people to observe the feast of pots.
When I came to the Areopagos, I stood
for trial, taking my place on one of the platforms,   940
while the leader of the Furies took the other stone.
I spoke to accusations over my mother's blood,
but Phoibos spoke in my behalf and rescued me,
and Pallas' arm counted an equal tale of votes.
Thus I emerged the winner from my murder trial.
Those Furies who were satisfied with judgment given
established a sanctuary at the place of trial.
But those who were not satisfied with the decree
kept driving me in chases that allowed no rest
until I came again to Apollo's holy ledge,   950
and, prone before his sanctuary, faint and starved,
swore then and there to die and break away my life
if Phoibos, who destroyed me, would not save me now.
Then from his golden tripod Phoibos spoke aloud
and sent me to this country, to reclaim the image
that fell from heaven, and settle it on Attic soil.
Then help me win that rescue which he has defined
for me. If we can seize the image of the goddess,
I shall be freed from madness, and in my oared ship
will take you to Mycenae, where your home will be.   960
But, O beloved sister, O my dearest one,
rescue your father's house and save me; all I have
is lost, and all the house of the Pelopidai,
unless we win the heavenly image of the god.

CHORUS Some deadly divine anger has boiled up against
the seed of Tantalos and drives it on, through pain.

IPHIGENEIA Even before you came I had always been eager
to be in Argos and, dear brother, to see you:
I wish what you wish: to release you from your trials,
and to restore our father's weakened house. I hold   970
no grudge, though he tried to kill me. This is what I wish.
For so my hand would not be guilty of your death,
and I would save our house. But I am afraid. How can I
escape the goddess and this tyrant, when he finds
the marble base is empty and the image gone?
Must I not then be killed? What could be my defense?
But if it all can be done in one single act,
if you can take both me and the image to the trim
ship, then the chance makes it an honorable risk.
If my part in this venture fails, then I must die;   980
but you, if you succeed in your part, might get home.
I do not try to avoid this, even if I must die
when once I have saved you. No. When the man of the
                    household dies
his loss is mourned. A woman does not count for much.

ORESTES I will not be the murderer both of my mother
and you. Her blood suffices. I would share your will
and try to live, but die together if we die.
If I myself can go there, I will take you home
as well; or else I must remain and die with you.
But hear my thought. If all this were against the will   990
of Artemis, how could Apollo have ordained
that I should take her image to Athena's ship?
That I should see your face? Combining all these thoughts,
I have good hope that we shall have our homecoming.

IPHIGENEIA How then can we contrive so that we do not die
and get what we desire? For this is the weakness
in our plans for homecoming, though the will is there.

ORESTES Could there be any way for us to kill the king?

IPHIGENEIA A terrible thought, for visitors to kill their host.

ORESTES Still, if it will save you and me, it should be dared.   1000

IPHIGENEIA I cannot do it, although I admire your zeal.

ORESTES What if you hid me secretly inside the shrine?

IPHIGENEIA So we should wait for dark to come, and then escape?

ORESTES Yes, since night is for thieves and daylight for the truth.

IPHIGENEIA But there are temple guards. We cannot hide from them.

ORESTES Alas, then, we are ruined. How can we escape?

IPHIGENEIA I have a new thought, and it might be the way out.

ORESTES What kind of thought? Share it with me, so I may know.

IPHIGENEIA I shall make artful use of your infirmities.

ORESTES Women are terribly clever in inventing schemes.   1010

IPHIGENEIA I will say you came from Argos as a matricide.

ORESTES Yes, use my sorrows, if you can turn them to our good.

IPHIGENEIA Thus, I shall say, we must not offer you to the goddess.

ORESTES What reason will you give? I think perhaps I see.

IPHIGENEIA That you are unclean. I'll make their piety serve their fear.

ORESTES But how, with all this, is the goddess-image stolen?

IPHIGENEIA I shall want to wash you clean in the waves of the sea.

ORESTES This leaves the image, which we sailed for, in the shrine.

IPHIGENEIA I will say, since you touched it, I must wash that too.

ORESTES Where in the sea? Do you mean where it joins a bay?   1020

IPHIGENEIA Right where your ship is tethered by its strands of rope.

ORESTES Will you or someone else carry the image down?

IPHIGENEIA I must. I alone am allowed to handle it.

ORESTES And what part shall our Pylades be given in this?

IPHIGENEIA We'll say his hands are stained with the same blood as yours.

ORESTES You plan this with or without the knowledge of the king?

IPHIGENEIA I must speak and persuade him, for I cannot hide.

ORESTES And then our ship is ready, and its oars are swift.

IPHIGENEIA Yes. Success in what follows must be in your hands.

ORESTES We need one more thing. These women must help keep   1030
the secret. Plead with them and find some words to win
their hearts. A woman has the power to work on pity.
The rest, perhaps—oh, may everything come out well!

IPHIGENEIA O dearest women, now I turn my eyes to you.
My fate is in your hands, whether I shall succeed
or come to nothing, lose the land where I was born,
and my dear brother, and my dearest sister too.
Let this be the beginning of my argument:
we are all women. We are loyal to each other,
surest protectors of all the interests we all share.   1040
Keep the secret of what we do, help us achieve
escape. Honor to her whose lips deserve their trust.
You see how we three, dearest friends, have all one chance
together, to come home again, or else to die.

If I am saved, I will save you, so that you share
my luck, and come to Hellas. You by your right hand
I supplicate, and you and you, you by your dear
cheek, by your knees, by all that's dearest in your homes,
mother and father, children of those who are mothers.
What is your answer? Who consents? Who will not?   1050
Speak. Who will do this? For if you refuse my plea,
then I am lost, and my unhappy brother too.

CHORUS Dear mistress, do not fear, but only save yourself.
I will keep silence about everything you do.
May great Zeus be my witness—and do all you say.

IPHIGENEIA May you never be sorry you said this, but be blessed.
              To ORESTES *and* PYLADES) It is time for you, and you, to go
                   inside the shrine.
The master of this country will come presently
to see if the strangers have been duly sacrified.

                   ORESTES *and* PYLADES *enter the temple.*

Artemis, queen, who saved me once at Aulis bay   1060
from my own father's terrible and murderous hand,
save me now also, and these men; or else the world
will never trust Apollo again, all through your fault.
Consent with grace to abandon this barbaric land
for Athens; here is no fit place for you to live
when you could have a city which the gods approve.

                   IPHIGENEIA *enters the temple.*

CHORUS Bird, sea bird by the rocky cliff,
          halcyon of the waters,
          yours is a song of sorrow,
          cry the gifted can understand,   1070
          mourning even in song your lost husband.
          I match your complaint with my own,
          I, a bird too, but wingless,

49

longing for gatherings of the Greeks,
longing for Artemis, bringer of birth,
who beside the Cynthian hill
dwells, and the slim-tressed palm tree,
sweet branching of laurel,
sacred growth of the olive gray,
friend to Leto in childbirth,   1080
by the pool with its spiral stream
where the swan, the singer of songs,
ministers to the Muses.

Many then were the streams of tears
down my cheeks coursing
when the towers of my city fell,
When I went away in the ship,
among the enemy's rowers and their spearmen.
I was traded dearly for gold
and came to a barbarous homeland.   1090
Here I serve Agamemnon's child,
priestess-maiden, who serves in turn
the goddess who slew the deer. She tends
sacrifices, but not of sheep.
I envy that sad life
that was grim throughout, for one grows used
to force, and can endure it.
It is the change that ruins.
Misfortune following happiness
comes as a crushing burden.   1100

You, our lady, the Argive ship
will carry home to Argos
as the wax-bound pipe of reed,
gift of Pan who ranges the hills,
whistles the oars onward,
and prophetic Apollo, making
music from his seven-stringed lyre,
brings you, singing, with fair landfall
to the shining country of Athens.

While I stay behind forsaken
you will go with the splashing oars
as, at the bow, stays hold the straining
sail that bellies over the bowsprit
on the speeding vessel.

But I would follow the shining course
where the sun flame goes with his horses,
and over the chambers of my own house
I would fold my wings on my back
and still them from their beating:
join the groups where once, as a girl   1120
and part of the marriage festival,
I danced away from my mother dear
to join the companies of my friends,
the contest of beauties,
rivalries of our glorious hair,
light-footed, and cast over my curls
and around my cheeks, shielding them from sunlight,
my bright and shimmering veil.

                                    Enter THOAS, *attended.*

THOAS Where is the keeper of this temple, the Greek woman?
      Has she yet dedicated the strangers? Do their bodies   1130
      shine with fire in the holy inner sanctuary?

CHORUS Here she is lord. She will give you a full account.

           Enter IPHIGENEIA *from the temple, with the wooden image*
                               of Artemis in her arms.

THOAS What is this?
      Why, daughter of Agamemnon, have you carried off
      the image from the fixed and holy pedestal?

IPHIGENEIA Do not step forward, lord! Keep your distance from it.

THOAS Iphigeneia, what has happened in the temple?

IPHIGENEIA   I spit it out. Hear me, O spirit of religion!

THOAS   What does this strange preamble mean? Tell me, more
            clearly.

IPHIGENEIA   Lord, the victims you captured for me are unclean.   1140

THOAS   What made this clear to you, or do you only guess?

IPHIGENEIA   The goddess-image turned about and faced away.

THOAS   All by herself, or did an earthquake turn her about?

IPHIGENEIA   All by herself; and closed the lids over her eyes.

THOAS   What was the cause? You mean, it was the strangers' guilt?

IPHIGENEIA   That, nothing else, for they have done an awful thing.

THOAS   Did they kill someone here on our barbarian shore?

IPHIGENEIA   They came already guilty of murder at home.

THOAS   Whom did they kill? I find myself longing to know.

IPHIGENEIA   They killed their mother. Both their sword-hands shared
            the act.   1150

THOAS   Apollo! None of our barbarians could have done it.

IPHIGENEIA   They were pursued and driven out from all Hellas.

THOAS   They are the cause, then, for your carrying out the image?

IPHIGENEIA   Yes, into holy daylight, to allay the taint.

THOAS   By what means did you learn about the strangers' guilt?

IPHIGENEIA I questioned them, after the image turned away.

THOAS Greece made you clever, so you understood this well.

IPHIGENEIA They thought they had a bait that would attract my mind.

THOAS They thought good news from Argos would endear your
heart?

IPHIGENEIA They said Orestes, my sole brother, prospered well.   1160

THOAS They hoped that you would save them; joyful at the news.

IPHIGENEIA They said my father was alive and prospering.

THOAS You took the goddess' side, though, as you ought to do?

IPHIGENEIA Yes, since I hate all Greece, the Greece that ruined me.

THOAS Tell me then, what must we do about these strangers?

IPHIGENEIA We must respect the law as it has been laid down.

THOAS We use your lustral waters, then? We use your sword?

IPHIGENEIA But first I wish to purify and make them clean.

THOAS In running springs, or in the waters of the sea?

IPHIGENEIA The sea washes away the ills of humankind.   1170

THOAS Thus they would fall as holier offerings to the god.

IPHIGENEIA And thus also it would be the better for me.

THOAS Do not the waves wash up about the very shrine?

IPHIGENEIA We need privacy. We have other tasks as well.

THOAS Take them where you will. I want no forbidden sight.

IPHIGENEIA I must also make clean the image of the goddess.

THOAS Yes, if the stain of mother-blood has sullied her.

IPHIGENEIA I would not otherwise have moved her from her base.

THOAS Your piety and forethought are commendable.

IPHIGENEIA Do you know then what I wish?

THOAS   It rests with you to give the
                                                    word.   1180

IPHIGENEIA Put these foreigners in chains.

THOAS   If they escaped, where could
                                                    they go?

IPHIGENEIA Greeks are never to be trusted.

THOAS   Go, you servants, get the chains.

IPHIGENEIA Have them also bring the strangers out to us.

THOAS   It shall be done.

IPHIGENEIA But put coverings on their heads.

THOAS   To keep pollution from the
                                                    sun.

IPHIGENEIA Send some of your henchmen with me.

THOAS   These shall be your
                                                    followers.

IPHIGENEIA Send one also who shall tell the city.

THOAS   What then shall he say?

IPHIGENEIA Tell all to remain indoors.

THOAS   For fear they meet the murderers?

IPHIGENEIA Yes, for such things are infectious.

THOAS (*to an attendant*)   Go and tell them, as she
                                                      said.

IPHIGENEIA None must look upon them.

THOAS   How you labor for our city's
                                                      good.

IPHIGENEIA Yes, and for my friends who most deserve it.

THOAS   That was meant
                                                      for me!   1190

IPHIGENEIA (And for all.)

THOAS   So all the Taurians admire and love you, as
                                  they should.

IPHIGENEIA Yes, remaining here before the temple of the goddess . . .

THOAS   Yes, what then?

IPHIGENEIA Cleanse the place with fire.

THOAS   So you may find it pure when
                                          you come back.

IPHIGENEIA When the strangers come out from the temple . . .

THOAS   Then
                                          what must I do?

IPHIGENEIA Hold your robe before your eyes.

THOAS   For fear pollution fall
                                             on me.

IPHIGENEIA If I seem to take too long a time . . .

THOAS   What limit should
                                             I set?

IPHIGENEIA Do not wonder.

THOAS   Go, and serve the goddess well. Your time
                             is yours.

IPHIGENEIA May this ritual only come out as I wish!

THOAS   Your prayers are
                                                mine.

IPHIGENEIA Now I see the strangers coming from the shrine. I see as well
            holy properties of the goddess, young lambs, so that, blood
                  by blood,   1200
            I can wash away the stain; I see the lighted torches, all
            that I ordered for the cleansing of the strangers and the god.
            Now I warn the citizens: avoid infection and stand clear,
            all who come to serve the temple, clean of hands before the
                  gods,
            all who come to join in marriage, or relief in giving birth:
            stand back all; take flight; begone, lest this pollution fall on
                  you.
            Maiden queen, daughter of Zeus and Leto: if I wash the
                  blood
            from these, and offer them where I ought to, you shall live in
                  a clean house,
            and we shall be high in fortune. Of the rest I do not speak,
            only, goddess, tell the gods and you, for you know more than
                  we.   1210

All leave except the CHORUS *and the (silent) attendants.*

CHORUS Beautiful was the child
   Leto bore in the grain-giving valley on Delos,
   A god with golden hair,
   skilled in the lyre, and with him the sister who glories
   in marksmanship with the bow. His mother
   carried him from the island ridge,
   leaving the storied place of birth,
   to the mountain, Parnassos,
   celebrant of Dionysos,
   place of the streaming torrents.   1220
   There a great snake, spangled
   of back, bright of eye,
   coiled in the dark shadow
   of laurel leafage,
   a monster out of primeval earth, controlled
   the chthonic oracle.
   You, Phoibos, still only a child
   in your mother's arms leaping,
   you killed it, and mounted the sacred oracle.
   You sit on the golden tripod, on the throne that never is false, 1230
   dealing out the prophetic answers to mortals
   from the inner chamber, neighbors to Kastalian springs,
      keeping
   your house at the world's center.

   When Apollo, going to Pytho,
   had driven Themis, daughter of Earth, from that sacred
   oracular place, then Earth
   produced the Dreams, nocturnal apparitions,
   and these to mortal multitudes divined
   things primeval, things of the time of telling,
   and what she would bring to pass,   1240
   by incubation in sleep under the dark ground.
   Earth, angry in her daughter's cause,
   took from Phoibos his privilege.
   But Lord Apollo ran on swift

feet to Olympos,
clung with his infant hand
to the throne of Zeus, pleading
that the grudge of the earth goddess be taken way
from the Pythian temple.
Zeus laughed, because his child   1250
had come in haste for the spoils with their golden treasures,
and shook his curls to affirm surcease of the night voices,
took away truth from what was shown men in night
            visions,
restored to Apollo his privileges,
and to mortals at the throne thronged with strangers gave
            confidence
in his oracular poems.

> Enter MESSENGER, who addresses at first not the CHORUS, but
> persons supposed to be behind the closed doors of
> the temple.

MESSENGER You temple guards and ministers who tend the altar,
            where is the lord of the land, Thoas, now to be found?
            Open the strongly nailed-together temple gates
            and summon from its fastnesses this country's king.   1260

CHORUS What is it? May I ask this uninvited question?

MESSENGER Those two young men have got loose, and are on their way,
            and Agamemnon's daughter plotted the escape.
            They are in flight from our country, and they have possession
            of the holy image, in the hull of a Greek ship.

CHORUS Your story is incredible. But the man you seek,
            the king of the country, left the temple in great haste.

MESSENGER Where did he go? He must be told of these events.

CHORUS We do not know. But go and see if you can find him,
            and when you do, then you can tell him all your story.   1270

MESSENGER   See, how untrustworthy is all the breed of women.
             You too have had some part in this conspiracy.

CHORUS   You are mad. What has the strangers' escape to do with us?
          Better make for the palace gates, and lose no time.

MESSENGER   No, not until the spokesman here gives me an answer,
             and tells me whether or not the king is in the shrine.
             Ho, you inside the temple, open up the doors,
             and tell your master that I stand within the gates
             burdened with bad news which I must announce to him.

THOAS   (*appearing as the doors open*) Who makes this outcry at
             the temple of the goddess   1280
          and batters at the doors and can be heard inside?

MESSENGER   Why did these women try to keep me off, and tell me
             that you were gone? You were in the building all the time.

THOAS   What could they have expected to gain by telling you that?

MESSENGER   I will tell you later about them, but hear from me
             what is immediate. The young woman who was here,
             Iphigeneia, who served the altar: she is gone
             out of the country with these strangers, and has taken
             the holy goddess-image. It was a treacherous plot.

THOAS   What are you saying? What could have inspired her to
             this?   1290

MESSENGER   Her purpose puzzles you. It was to save Orestes.

THOAS   Whom do you mean? Her brother, of the Tyndarid line?

MESSENGER   Yes, and the very man who was to be sacrificed.

THOAS   Astonishing event! How else could I describe it?

59

MESSENGER Do not bother your mind with that, but hear my story;
        when you have heard and studied the facts, then you can
           plan
        the best way of pursuit to run the strangers down.

THOAS Well argued. Tell your story. They have no short course
        to run, before they can escape my force of arms.

MESSENGER When we had reached the sea shore, where Orestes' ship   1300
        lay moored within its hiding-place, then we, the ones
        you sent to guard the foreigners and hold their chains,
        were nodded to by Agamemnon's daughter, and told
        to stand off out of the way, since she was occupied
        with mysteries of flame and lustral sacrifice.
        She herself held the bonds behind the strangers' backs
        and went away. All this was matter for suspicion,
        but had to be accepted by your servants, lord.
        At last, so we might think something was being done,
        she raised the cry, and sang incomprehensible   1310
        songs of magic, as if she were washing bloodstains away.
        But when we felt we had been sitting there too long,
        a fear came into our minds; the strangers might have got
           free,
        murdered the priestess, and made off, and sailed away.
        Still, fear of what we must not look at kept us sitting
        in silence, till at last everyone there agreed
        that we must go and find them, though it was forbidden.
           And there we saw the hull of a Hellenic ship,
        winged with oars, which were dipped in the water, ready
           to go,
        and fifty sailors at the benches with their oars.   1320
        We saw the young men, liberated from their bonds,
        and there were sailors, standing at the stern of the ship,
        who hastily pulled up the cables with their hands.
        Others with poles held fast the prow, others drew up
        the anchor to the cathead, others let down ladders
        into the sea, for those three Greeks to come aboard.
           We cast out all consideration when we saw

the treacherous games they played, laid hands on the Greek
      girl,
and seized the cables. We reached through the rudder-ports
and tried to drag the steering oars from the stout ship.   1330
And words came out: "What do you mean, to steal and
      carry
our images and priestesses out of the country?
You are depriving us of her. What is your name?"
He said: "If you must know, I am Orestes, son
of Agamemnon, and her brother. Thus I take
my sister to that home from which she once was lost."
In spite of this we kept our hold on the Greek girl
and tried to force her to come back to you with us.
Hence came these terrible bruises you see on my face,
since neither they nor we had steel weapons to use,   1340
but there were fist-fights, in which we were sorely battered.
Also, these two young men used their feet in the fighting
and drove them home to ribs and stomach; thus, if one
of us closed with them, he was knocked helpless at once.
Wearing the marks their fists had left upon our faces,
we fled back to the sea cliffs, some with bloody wounds
upon their heads, while others had been hit in the eyes.
There, standing on the high ground, we thought to fight
      with them
to better advantage, and we pelted them with stones;
still, archers stationed on the stern deck held us off   1350
with showers of arrows, driving us still further back.
Meanwhile, a difficult surf was washing the ship ashore,
and there was danger that anyone might be submerged.
Orestes caught his sister up on his left shoulder,
waded into the sea, and sprang upon the ladder,
and set her down aboard the well-constructed ship,
together with the thing that fell from the sky, the image
of Artemis. From amidships, someone cried aloud:
"You mariners of Greece, seize your oars in your hands,
whiten the water. We have all that for whose sake   1360
we ever came to this inhospitable sea
and passed within the entrance of the Clashing Rocks."

The sailors, answering him with a hearty roar,
lashed at the water. While the ship was still inside
the bay, she went straight on, but when she passed the
          mouth,
she came to grips with the rough sea, and had to fight,
for the hard wind fell on her in a sudden squall
and took her sails aback. The men still struggled on,
bracing their heels to fight it, but the contrary sea
forced the ship back again toward land. Then Agamemnon's   1370
daughter stood up and prayed, saying: "O Leto's child,
bring me, your priestess, safely back again to Greece
from this barbaric country, and forgive my theft.
You, Artemis, love your own brother; thus I too
think it is right that I should love my family."
      The sailors blessed the girl's prayer with a cheerful song,
and with their sleeves rolled up and arms bared all their
          length
plied their oars to the rhythm of the coxswain's chant;
but, little by little, the ship was forced back to the rocks.
Then some of us ran into the sea and waded out,   1380
and others made fast looping ropes to hold them with,
and I was sent away, to come direct to you
and tell you, lord, about what has been happening there.
But go there, taking bonds and halters in your hands.
Unless all wind suddenly vanishes on the sea,
the foreigners have no hope of escaping us.
Holy Poseidon watches over Ilion still,
lord of the sea, ever opposed to Pelops' line,
and he, it seems, will give up Agamemnon's son
a prisoner to your hands and to your citizens';   1390
with him his sister, whose ingratitude is proved
toward Artemis; who rescued her; whom she betrayed.

CHORUS Oh, poor Iphigeneia; with your brother, you
        shall be brought back into our master's hands, and die.

THOAS   Oh all you citizens of our barbarian land,
        haste, will you not? And put the harness on your horses,

gallop along the shore and meet them as they land
from their Greek ship, and with the help of Artemis
and your good speed, you will hunt out these godless men.
Sailors, drag your swift-rowing ships down to the sea.   1400
So we shall ride them down by water and by land,
and after we have caught them we shall throw them down
the steep cliff, or impale their bodies on sharp spikes.
As for you women implicated in this plot,
at some time later, when I find leisure to spare,
I'll punish you, but now the urgent task at hand
has occupied us, and we have no time to rest.

ATHENA *appears aloft, above the temple.*

ATHENA King Thoas: What pursuit is this? Where do you mean
to carry it? Listen to what Athena says.
Call off your streaming soldiery. Stop the pursuit.   1410
By destiny and the decrees of Loxias
Orestes came here, fleeing from the Furies' rage,
to find his sister and to take her home to Argos,
and carry the sacred image to my own country,
for thus they shall be quitted of the present pains.
This is my speech, Thoas, to you. You mean to kill
Orestes when you catch him on the stormy shore;
but even now Poseidon, to please me, has made
the heaving waters calm, so that his ship can sail.

  And now, Orestes, study my commands to you,   1420
for you, though far away, can hear the goddess speak.
Proceed, taking the statue with you, and your sister.
But when you come to Athens the divinely built,
you will find there is a place in Attica, the last
before the border, across from the Karystian mount;
a sacred place, which is called Halai by my people.
There found a temple (and install the image there),
named from the Tauric country and your wanderings,
when you labored hard, ranging through the land of Greece,
stung by the Furies. People for the rest of time   1430
shall sing her praise as Artemis Tauropolos.

Establish there this custom: at the festival,
to atone for your uncompleted sacrifice,
let a sword be held to a man's throat, and blood be drawn,
for religion's sake, so that the goddess may have her rights.
Iphigeneia, on the sacred terraced ground
of Brauron, you must keep the keys for Artemis.
There, when you die, you shall be buried. They shall bring
to you in dedication the fine-woven clothes
which wives, who die in the pangs of childbirth, leave behind   1440
in their houses.
                Thoas, now I charge you to release
these Greek women from your country and send them
        home,
because of their good will.
                    Orestes, once before
I saved you on the Areopagos, with my
judgment of even votes. The custom now shall be
acquittal of the accused whenever the score is tied.
Now, son of Agamemnon, sail, convey your sister
away from this country.
                And you, Thoas, cease to rage.

THOAS Goddess Athena, when the gods speak to a man
and he will not believe them, then he is a fool.   1450
I am not angry with Orestes and his sister
though he has taken the image. What honor is there
in setting ourselves against the gods, who have the power?
Let them go to your country, let them take the image
and there establish it with all good auspices.
So also I shall send these women back to Greece
and happiness. Such is your will and your command.
I shall disband the force I raised against the Greeks,
and my ships, goddess, in accordance with your will.

ATHENA Good. You, and the gods also, yield to what must be.   1460
Then go, you winds, and waft the son of Agamemnon
to Athens. I myself shall go along with you
and guard the holy image of Artemis, my sister.

CHORUS Go, fortunate, numbered among the saved,
           in good fortune, go.
           O Pallas Athena, worshipful
           among immortals and mortals too,
           we shall do all you would have us do,
           for what we have heard is full of joy
           and beyond all hope.   1470
           O Victory, great and august, control,
           if you will, my life,
           and continue to crown me with garlands.

NOTES AND GLOSSARY

NOTES

The cast: The rules for the highly competitive tragic productions allowed each dramatist only three actors for spoken parts, in addition to the chorus. They were called in order of importance *protagonist, deuteragonist,* and *tritagonist.* There was also an allowance of non-speaking parts; we do not know how many. The distribution of parts for this play would certainly have given Iphigeneia to the protagonist and Orestes to the deuteragonist; the total distribution was probably somewhat as follows:

> *Protagonist:* Iphigeneia, Athena
> *Deuteragonist:* Orestes, Herdsman, Messenger
> *Tritagonist:* Pylades, Thoas

When Orestes and Pylades are brought into the presence of Thoas, Thoas and Pylades are on together. But Pylades (like Orestes) has his head covered! In any case, of course, the actors changed their identity by changing not only their costumes, but also their masks.

The scene: The shrine, or temple, of Artemis stands on a slightly raised platform, and is approached by a wide flight of steps. It has a single door. The roof is gabled, with an open space at the peak. In front of the temple is an altar, blood-stained and hung with human skulls. At the foot of the steps is a round level space, the orchestra. Paved walks to left and right lead out of the theater. These, plus the temple door, are the only entrances. Stage right, to the audience's left, is understood by convention to lead to and from the country and the sea; stage left, audience right, to and from the town. All entrances and exits, except in and out of the temple, are made by means of these entrances, which means that to reach the level of the temple the persons must mount the steps. Iphigeneia remains on the temple level throughout until she comes down to lead her procession off. The Chorus remains on the lower level throughout.

A NOTE ON THE PARTS OF TRAGEDY

The conventional terms are derived from Aristotle: *Prologue:* everything which precedes the entrance of the Chorus. *Parodos:* the entrance lines of the Chorus. *Episode:* all that takes place between two choral songs. *Stasimon:* all choral songs except in the *parodos* and *kommos* (a section partly in lyric meters in which one or more of the actors and the Chorus take part; sometimes substituted for *stasimon*). *Exodos:* everything which follows the last *stasimon*.

Thus the "acts" of the play are *prologue,* the *episodes,* and *exodos.* In Aristotelian terms, the prologue to our play would include the dialogue between Orestes and Pylades (67-122). But the term is often applied to the monologue with which Euripides regularly opened his plays, where the speaker identifies himself or herself and brings the story up to date, as Iphigeneia does in 1-66. Aristophanes ridiculed Euripides for his prologues, considering them factual, genealogical, and pedestrian.

NOTES ON THE TEXT

1-5 A brief outline of the family tree, in part:

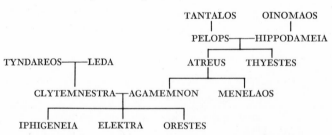

2 *with his swift chariot* Pelops won Hippodameia by defeating her father in a chariot race (actually, a pursuit). Oinomaos (see Glossary) was killed, with the aid of his daughter and Myrtilos, his treacherous charioteer. This and other crimes and betrayals in the family history are ignored in this account; but see 186-95 and note.

15-25 Kalchas, the diviner of Agamemnon, is always made responsible for the advice to sacrifice Iphigeneia; and Odysseus is always made the agent of the treacherous plot. Iphigeneia speaks of both with hatred (522-6), as do other persons in the plays of Euripides, who disliked both sooth-sayers and clever politicians.

20 *the loveliest thing* Elsewhere, Agamemnon is made to enrage Artemis by claiming to surpass her in archery. In this version, the vow must have been made in the year Iphigeneia was born, and remained unfulfilled until she was of marriageable age—fourteen or fifteen years at least. Do we have a trace of a version in which an *infant* Iphigeneia was sacrificed?

21 *goddess who brings light* If this means Artemis as *moon*-goddess, it is the earliest case of this identification known to me. Normally, Selene, not Artemis, is the moon, just as Helios, not Apollo, is the sun. It is inter-esting that Euripides, in his fragmentary *Phaëthon*, seems to offer the earliest attested identification of Apollo and the sun. *Phaëthon* was probably written at about the same time as *Iphigeneia in Tauris*.

30 *to this land of the Taurians* There never was any country, real or mythical, called Tauris. The general acceptance of the title *Iphigeneia in Tauris* is due to a combination of accidents. Greek works have been conven-tionally described by Latin titles, Latin being the universal language of western scholars. In Latin, *Iphigeneia in Tauris* is perfectly correct; but what it means is "Iphigeneia among the *Tauri*," that is, Taurians. The analogy of the correct title, *Iphigeneia in Aulis*, which almost rhymes with our title, has further encouraged its acceptance.

31 *the barbarian.* The Greeks called all non-Greeks barbarian. They also, quaintly, make barbarians call themselves barbarians (for instance, 1395). Pos-sibly the terms should always be capitalized.

42-60 The dream is false, or misinterpreted. In the hymn about Apollo, dreams, once genuinely prophetic, were deprived of their truthfulness by Zeus (1253).

60 *Strophios had no children* Strophios married Anaxibia, sister of Agamemnon; any child of his would be a first cousin (see 895-900). If Pylades had not yet been born when Iphigeneia was "sacrificed," he would have to be at least fourteen years younger than she, though married to her full sister. I find this a little awkward, but Euripides insists on it. It en-ables him to have the Herdsman's use of "Pylades" (241, 277, 313,

484) mean nothing to Iphigeneia while it does mean something to us, audience or readers: a kind of irony, which plays to the audience at the expense of the dramatic character.

112 *the wooden image*   We are to think of it as small, light, thus easily portable.

123-227 *Parodos including kommos.*

123 *Silence, oh silence*   They expect a religious ceremony, during the course of which no one must speak, for fear of evil omens. These lines are addressed to any of the populace who may be within hearing (compare 1395). The Chorus then address Artemis, by one of her foreign names, and finally, Iphigeneia.

124. *Clashing Rocks*   These are referred to again and again in the play. They are also sometimes called the Black Rocks (736) without any apparent distinction. As generally told in legend, they stood at the entrance to the Black Sea. They had moved together and crushed ships trying to pass, until the *Argo* got through on its way to the Golden Fleece and, in so doing, miraculously put an end to that miracle. Sometimes in this play Euripides seems to locate them in their traditional place. Sometimes, as here, he writes as if they were very close to the scene of action. There were two Bosporuses, one at the entrance to the Black Sea, one near the Taurian land, often confused. Principally, Euripides may be using these rocks simply as a badge to label the whole Black Sea region.

159-73 The libations are the best she can do. If she could be at his tomb, she could offer a lock of her hair.

175 *the Asian strain, the barbarian dirge*   Why Asian, why barbarian? The women are Greek, and dirges are Greek; there is one in almost every tragedy. Perhaps this only means that Greeks considered barbarians to be more emotional than Greeks.

180-95 Lament for the house of Atreus. After Pelops defeated Oinomaos with the help of Myrtilos, the charioteer (see 1-5 and note), Pelops hurled Myrtilos to death from his chariot. But the MS. reading is uncertain, and the chariot referred to may be the chariot of the sun.

    The golden lamb symbolized the kingship of Argos or Mycenae. Atreus and Thyestes quarreled over it. Theyestes, with the help of

Aërope, the unfaithful wife of Atreus, obtained possession of the lamb; Atreus in revenge tricked Thyestes into eating his own children. In horror at these acts, the Sun, who had formerly risen in the west and set in the east, reversed his course. These events are only a part of the lurid history of the house of Tantalos, and are touched on here with a relatively light hand (compare Aeschylus in *Agamemnon*). This is one of those grand and awful family sagas whose material is the very stuff of tragedy. Other great tragic houses are those of Laios in Thebes, of Amphiaraos and Alkmaion in Argos, and of Oineus in Aitolia.

196-227 Lament by Iphigeneia for Iphigeneia herself, not her house.

209 *a bride cursed* A princess would expect to marry, and she expected Achilles, the most brilliant of all.

214 *I do not dance* A princess even if not married would take part in the decorous pastimes of Greek girls, not the outlandish pastimes of the Taurians.

228-383 First episode.

241 *Pylades* See note on 60.

246 *What have oxherds to do with the sea?* The aristocratic heroes and heroines of tragedy are sometimes curt with rustics and underlings (Hippolytos in *Hippolytos*; Hektor in *Rhesos*; Elektra in Euripides, *Elektra*).

250-1 *Never yet . . . upon the altar* There is a real problem here and it connects with another problem. What duties have been performed by Iphigeneia since her arrival in the Taurian land, and on whom has she performed them? Here she states positively that no Greeks have been sacrificed yet. Elsewhere she certainly implies that they have; otherwise 38-41 is meaningless. The altar has been stained with Greek blood (72-5). Iphigeneia has always pitied any Greeks who came her way (336-9); this makes no sense if no Greeks have come, or if those who have have been spared. See also 269. Furthermore, the kind Greek who wrote her letter for her (574-9) did not deliver it and would, in the context, certainly have been put to death.

Some editors have dealt with the problem by deleting these lines as spurious. We are left with a choice. We must assume an idiotic interpolator, or else a careless author. Idiotic interpolators have no doubt existed, though perhaps not in quite such numbers as some editors of Greek texts would have us believe. But a careless author seems the more likely when we face the connected problem and ask ourselves what part Iphigeneia played in the sacrifices. She is made to tell us twice, explicitly, that she merely consecrates the victims, who are then dispatched by male executioners (38-41, 614-16; at 714 she addresses such people). But "he did not think my *hand*/ was murderous" (577) suggests an Iphigeneia who wielded a weapon, and the wish expressed in 434 implies this. 856-7 is more explicit: "death at my hands/ which would have torn you." Then finally there is Thoas to Iphigeneia with "your sword" (1167). Here are too many contradictions to be removed by emendation or excision. I can only suppose something like this. At one point in composition Euripides entertained the concept of an Iphigeneia who actually wielded a knife against her brother, just as her father had wielded a knife against her. Then, committed to mere consecration, he failed to remove all traces of the other version. Or vice versa. Similarly, he might have delayed his decision as to whether or not Orestes and Pylades were the first Greeks to be brought to sacrifice.

262-6 Ino, daughter of Kadmos and wife of Athamas, leapt into the sea with her son, Learchos, in her arms. They turned into sea deities named Leukothea and Palaimon. "Nurslings dear to Nereus" suggests Achilles, son of the Nereid, thus grandson of Nereus. The Dioscuri are the Heavenly Twins. (See Glossary.) Throughout this narrative we are made to feel the physical superiority of the Greek heroes to the Taurian herdsmen.

267 *a rough man*   A similar wise guy who had been in the city incites the herdsmen to violence in the *Bacchae*.

282 Reading *achthos* (Greverus, Platnauer) for *ochthon* (MMS., Murray).

283 *There was nothing there*   Aeschylus in the *Eumenides* used the Furies as his Chorus. In this play also at 939-49 a physical presence of the Furies is implied.

338-49 One may doubt whether Iphigeneia is meant to be as fierce as she says she is. She is full of sympathy for the two young men as soon as she confronts them. But in tragedy all virtuous women hate Helen, and the Chorus echo her sentiments about this (428-36).

361 The theme of Death and the Maiden. Hades is a ravisher.

378-80 The crudities of accepted myth. Tantalos was said to have cut up his son, Pelops, and offered him to the gods, who, however, restored him to life.

384-456 First *stasimon*.

384-90 The meeting-place of two seas is usually taken as the Bosporus, joining the Sea of Marmora to the Black Sea. Here Io, in the form of a cow, crossed over and made her way ultimately to Egypt. The story is told by Aeschylus in the *Suppliants* and *Prometheus*. In the poets, however, whose great strength is not geography, this Bosporus is often confused with the Cimmerian (Crimean) Bosporus, near the land of the Taurians, and both in turn are confused with the Black or Clashing Rocks. (See note on 124.)

387 *Euxine* This name for the Black Sea properly means "hospitable" (a propitiatory name to ingratiate a surly body of water). Sometimes it seems in this play to be called *axenos*, "inhospitable," but the readings are not always certain.

390-2 That is, they are Greeks, but what Greek place is their home? Sparta (its river is the Eurotas) or Thebes (its river is Dirke)?

397-409 Only desperate need or lust for money would induce sane men to go on long sea voyages. This is the unromantic thought expressed here; it goes back to Hesiod and Solon.

410-27 These lines describe the coast between the entrance to the Black Sea and the land of the Taurians. Phineus was the king tormented by Harpies. For the Nereids, see Glossary.

425 *the white strand* The myth was that Achilles after death was transported to the island of Leuke opposite the mouth of the Danube, where, fleet footed, he continued to race. Herodotos, writing serious geography, speaks of a "Race course of Achilles" on the mainland. The Chorus in their ode refer to Achilles as a known hero of myth, although they presumably do not know yet that he is dead (528-9).

428-36 See the note on 338-49.

458-634 *Second episode.*

493 It would be undramatic if Orestes gave away his name too soon. No enemy can exult over his death if no one knows who has died. Hence Orestes' testy responses to what he considers misplaced and useless sympathy.

499 *Argos* Here Orestes says he is from Argos, at 501 that he is from Mycenae, as if they were synonymous. See ARGOS in Glossary. At 795 Iphigeneia names both Argos and Nauplia.

503 *involuntary voluntary* The "sophistic cleverness" of Euripides. Voluntary because his city had not exiled him; involuntary, because the Furies drove him, and he had not wished to leave his city.

513 *bad news for one of my family* The troubles of the whole family, in this generation, originated in the flight, or (to be Euripidean) voluntary rape, of Helen. Thus the reference could be either to Orestes himself or, if the dead can be brought in, Agamemnon, or even Iphigeneia. Note that Euripides here ignores the version of Helen's disappearance which he adopted in *Helen* and introduced at the end of *Elektra*.

522-7 Kalchas and Odysseus. See note on 15-25.

529 *His marriage at Aulis* A strange answer for Orestes to give to Iphigeneia's question, and in fact a *non sequitur*. The marriage was a swindle, but would Achilles be any the more alive if he had married Iphigeneia? But these lines are composed as if mostly from the heroine's point of view. To her he is above all else the falsely promised bridegroom.

534-5 The word, *eudaimon*, used by both speakers, could mean either "great and powerful" or "ultimately fortunate." But Euripides is very likely thinking of *Iliad* III. 182, where Priam says: "O son of Atreus, blessed, child of fortune and favor."

544 Reading *thanōn* (variant MS. reading) rather than *ktanōn* (Murray, with MS. authority).

554 *one daughter, Elektra, a girl still young* The names and number of Agamemnon's daughters vary considerably in epic and tragedy. The strange thing here is that Orestes speaks as if his sister were unmarried (the word used, *parthenos*, usually means "virgin"). But she already is

married to Pylades, as Orestes says later, 893. Another contradiction? Rather, the detail of explaining about Pylades, who is silently present, would complicate the progress of this question-and-answer.

561-7 Later, in the mythic hymn about Apollo, we shall be told that dreams are indeed false prophets, but Apollo a true one.

570-88 The rule must be understood to be that, out of any group of more than one, *one* person must be sacrificed. Iphigeneia, presumably, is illiterate.

635-46 Short *kommos,* which occupies the place where we would normally find a *stasimon.*

647-1066 Third episode.

664 *I must also share your death* Perhaps it would not be reasonable to expect Pylades to offer to die *instead* of Orestes; but that would be a more useful offer than this one, to die *with* him.

700-4, 712 Since Apollo is very soon going to be vindicated, this baiting of him is not so much Euripidean challenge of the gods as dramatic tact. See Introduction II.

756 Reading *tōn te sōn* (Haupt, approved by Platnauer, adopted by Murray in his translation though not in his text) for *tōn theōn* (MSS.).

769 I give all the line to Iphigeneia, with Platnauer. The MSS. are confused about attribution.

779 Beginning the famous recognition scene. A later dramatist, Polyeidos (as we learn from Aristotle), made the key line Orestes' remark: "So I was fated to be sacrificed, like my sister." *She* would then recognize *him.* Aristotle (*Poetics*) mentions this later variant with approval; but the handing over of the letter before our eyes is a sure dramatic touch.

782-801 It is normal in the scene of recognition of the long-lost loved one to have the recognized character reluctant and skeptical.

795 See the note on 499.

803, 807 See the note on 180-95.

817 *in your own . . . room* No young male, if not one of the household, would have been allowed in her bedchamber.

880-6 Strange as it seems by later standards, these are the last lines Pylades speaks; but he must stand by, wordless, for almost 200 more lines.

898 See 60 and note there.

902-5 Neat and very cool. See Introduction.

917-64 This is a considerable narrative speech, to be undramatically delivered at a time when the audience, like Pylades, might have been chafing to hear plans for a quick, efficient escape. I take it that Euripides felt it necessary to detail the compromise by which he stitched together the version that had Orestes acquitted and set free at Athens (Aeschylus) and the one that made him have to go and rescue Artemis (and, as it turned out, his sister) from the Taurians. Like the jurors, the Furies themselves were divided. (946-56).

924 *for Ares* Hence the name Areopagus ('hill of Ares"). Ares had murdered Halirrhothios, son of Poseidon.

925-6 *nobody in the city* What follows is a good example of the etiological myth, a story told to explain a fact or custom. If a man, however morally innocent, were guilty of bloodshed or corruption, none, for fear of pollution, could share hearth or board with him. The hospitable Athenians, so as to entertain Orestes without suffering themselves, decreed that every man should eat by himself; as, at the Feast of the Pots in historical times, they continued to do.

940 At Athens, the accused and accuser faced each other standing on two rocks, the stone of *Hybris* (outrageous violence) and that of *Anaideia* (relentlessness); or, to simplify it, crime and punishment.

983-4 *When the man . . . count for much* In *Iphigeneia in Aulis* the heroine puts this Athenian sentiment even more forcibly: better for one man to live than ten thousand women. But Orestes, at least, will not even consider it.

999 *kill their host* Not much of a host to Orestes and Pylades; but she too would be implicated in such a murder, and Thoas has been kind to her.

1010 *terribly clever* Certainly in the corresponding scene in *Helen* the heroine is sharper than Menelaos; and one could make a good case for contending that Euripides really thought women were cleverer and quicker than men. But the compliment is as much left-handed as right-handed; the term I have so translated indicates unwilling admiration of something sinister.

1012 In the corresponding scene in *Helen*, 1050-2, the hero also *consents* to something unpleasant, if it will serve the purpose; namely, the ill-omened pretense that he is dead.

1045 *I will save you* How she intends to set about doing this is not clear. It takes a divine appearance and command to save these women.

1049 *children of those who are mothers* According to Platnauer, most editors have rejected the line, on the ground that the Chorus is composed of virgins (the "maidenly step" of 130). That seems hardly enough evidence; the same word (*parthenos*) is used of Elektra, who is married (see note on 554). At 1120-8 they speak of the experience of a young girl, but they are remembering the past, perhaps remote as well as immediate.

1067-1128 Second *stasimon*. This well-known ode became much beloved by English-speaking readers through Gilbert Murray's now unfashionable but still beautiful rendering. Unfortunately the text of the second half is in very bad shape, and the meaning some of the time quite uncertain.

1068 *halcyon* The bird is Alkyone, wife of Keyx, who mourned for her lost husband until she turned into a bird; some say kingfisher, but this is doubtful. So the Chorus, too, mourn their lost country.

1074-1080 But why, particlarly and exclusively, Delos, place of the Cynthian hill, where Leto gave birth to Apollo and Artemis? Delos had been a festal gathering-place of the Ionians; but the association here seems to be with the birthplace of Artemis, goddess of childbirth.

1082 *the swan* Apollo's bird, whose final song is fabulous.

1084-90 The women remember when their city fell and they were taken prisoner and sold as slaves; something which happened to Greek women at the hands of Greeks several times during the late phase of Euripides' career, most notoriously at the capture of Melos by the Athenians in 416 B.C.

1097 Reading *kamnei* (John Milton according, according to Platnauer) for *kamneis* (older MSS., Murray).

1101-5 The women wistfully contrast their fate with that of the fugitives. But whom do they mean by "you"? One would expect them to address Iphigeneia, and the mention of the Argive ship suggests that "home" is Argos. But at the end (1109) the destination is Athens, as if for Artemis. The destination of Iphigeneia at this point is Argos, and she is going home. Further, the term *potnia*, "my lady," used at the beginning, is mostly reserved for goddesses; and to have two gods in person lending their music to time the rowers is more suitable for the transportation of a goddess than the stealthy flight of a human heroine. There probably is a real confusion here, arising perhaps from the latent relationship, even identity, of heroine and goddess (see note on 1424-41). I have left it vague.

1112 Readings and sense are confused and doubtful.

1115-20 Not in the halcyon theme at the beginning of this ode—for there the women lament with or like the halcyon—but here, do they wish for wings that would carry them across the world and—who knows—back into girlhood again?

1124 *contest of beauties*   Beauty contests for real girls, not just trios of goddesses, are attested by Alkaios and others. But here, I think, the girls merely rival each other in beauty.

1129-1210 Fourth *episode*.

1138 *I spit it out*   That is, I want nothing to do with it. Word for action.

1151 *None of our barbarians*   In *Medea*, Jason says of Medea's murders: "No Greek woman would have done it."

1167 *your sword*   See the note on 250.

1190-1 See Introduction I. The fatuity of the poor gulled pious barbarian outwitted by a Greek woman, clever on both counts, is evident in every line. I do not believe Thoas is in love with the unmarriageable priestess; rather, he is pleased with her gratitude and proud of her friendship.

1191 Three syllables missing. Thoas' answer almost calls for something like this.

1195 *your eyes* Pollution infected the eye of the beholder as it infected the sun, the eye of the world (1185).

1211-56 Third *stasimon*. A hymn to Apollo. The contents in brief are: Leto carried her infant son from Delos to his other, prophetic, home at Pytho (Delphi) on the lower slopes of Mount Parnassos. There was already an oracle there, in charge of Themis, daughter of Earth, and guarded by a great snake, the original Python, a son of Earth. When the snake was slain and Themis driven from the throne of prophecy, Earth took it away again and established Dreams as prophetic agents. But the still-infant Apollo ran with his claims to Zeus, his father, who, amused by his child's truly Olympian rapacity, restored the rights to him.

1218-19 *Parnassos, celebrant of Dionysos* Delphi (Pytho) on the lower slopes belonged to Apollo, but the great mountain itself to Dionysos, whose revels were held higher up. So the mountain itself was celebrant at these sacred revels. Mountains in central Greece and Boeotia, such as Parnassos, Helikon, and Kithairon, were regarded, especially in Boeotian thought, as personalities.

1227 The baby killing the monstrous snake recalls, of course, Herakles; sometimes Apollo's protégé, sometimes his rival, sometimes perhaps his *alter ego*.

1237 *Dreams* These were used in divination. But Iphigeneia's dream, misinterpreted to be sure, was false. Apollo's prophecies, doubted, proved true. Despite his predatory ways, Apollo may here be thought of as advancing culture and civilization over the inarticulate early religion.

1257-1473 *Exodos* with theophany or *deus ex machina*.

1257 Messenger There may be more than one messenger in a tragedy, but the Messenger *par excellence* is the one who arrives late in the play to narrate the catastrophe or decisive event (though in this play the action is not decided until the god appears).

1275 *the spokesman* The word means "interpreter." In civilized Egypt, for example, there would probably be bilingual guides who showed Greek and other tourists around the wonderful sights, particulary the sanctuaries. It is rather quaint to think of such an official at the untouristy, not to say anti-tourist, sanctuary of the Taurians; yet that may be indicated. Uncertain, I have hedged. Murray thinks the "spokesman" is a stick or club with which the Messenger will hammer on the door and force an answer.

1275-9 See Introduction II. We must have this story. But it does, though full of naturalistic detail, strain credulity. For it will appear within the speech that the two Greek men, hampered by a young woman and an image, whom they have to protect and to carry some of the time, have already given the king's men enough trouble to justify calling out the whole army at once. There will not be just two Greeks but a whole shipload to deal with. See also notes on 1340, 1395, 1408.

1322-6 After attempting in vain to extract a reasonable reading from the manuscript tradition, I have adopted Platnauer's combination of previous suggestions, although it involves transposing one line and making five other changes. Platnauer also would follow Weil and postulate a lacuna in the middle of 1349 (Greek) or between 1322 and 1323 (English). This would make the construction smoother, but I would rather refrain from more surgery than is absolutely necessary. Greeks moored their ships on a beach with the prow facing outward. There were three ways of holding the ship in place: anchors or anchor-stones at both bow and stern and, when these were pulled in, poles.

1340 *neither they nor we had steel weapons* It is once more a strain on our credulity when we are asked to believe that Thoas' men were not armed. This may at least, however, be why Iphigeneia explicitly asked Thoas to have Orestes and Pylades bound; had they not been, their guards must have been armed. (bronze)

1387-90 *Holy Poseidon* In the *Iliad*, Apollo is the chief defender of Troy; in Euripides, Poseidon.

1396 *haste* Here at last is that urgency one might have expected at 1298 or thereabouts.

1408 Athena.   Euripides usually closes with the appearance of a god. The god ties up loose ends, explains the action, corrects misunderstanding, and predicts the future—including, usually, the establishment of a cult. The god does not always solve a dramatic problem, though he may do so.

Why did not Euripides simply let the ship escape (as in *Helen*) and have Athena perform her other functions, enlighten and pacify Thoas, and save the women of the Chorus? He seems deliberately to have painted himself into a corner so that divine aid is necessary; possibly because the ultimate benevolence of heaven has been doubted throughout the play. In a happy-ending tragedy the gods must be, in the end, benign.

And why Athena rather than Artemis? Because Artemis is being rescued, in person, in the form of her image?

1418 *Poseidon, to please me*   Thus in the *Trojan Women* Poseidon and Athena drop their differences and work together (not, this time, for benevolent purposes).

1424-41 The establishment of the cult, or cults. Two places are involved: Halai and Brauron, on the southeast coast of Attica, a few miles apart. Artemis Tauropolos was worshiped at Halai; Artemis, sometimes called Iphigeneia, at Brauron. We are told sometimes that the Taurian image of Artemis was at one, sometimes at the other. Euripides seems to be trying to do justice to two rival claims. The imitation of human sacrifice goes, here, with the image (1433-5); Iphigeneia shall serve Artemis the goddess of childbirth (1436-41). Throughout here, one may discern the original identity of goddess and heroine.

1471-3 These last three lines also conclude Euripides' *Phoenician Women* and *Orestes*. They sound like an appeal to the judges to vote favorably for the poet who wrote these lines.

GLOSSARY

ACHILLES, son of Peleus and Thetis, pretended fiancé of Iphigeneia.

ACHAIANS, epic and dramatic name for Hellenes or Greeks.

AGAMEMNON, son of Atreus, father of Orestes and Iphigeneia, murdered by his wife, Clytemnestra.

AMPHITRITE, goddess, wife of Poseidon.

AREOPAGOS, the hill of Ares.

ARES, god of war, worshiped particularly in Thrace.

ARGIVE, belonging to Argos.

ARGOS, city in southern Greece. In Aeschylus, Argos is the city of Agamemnon and Menelaos. Elsewhere, the claims of Argos are disputed by Mycenae. Euripides honors both.

ARTEMIS, daughter of Leto, sister of Apollo, worshiped with human sacrifice among the Taurians.

ATREUS, son of Pelops, father of Agamemnon and Menelaos.

AULIS, port in central Greece, gathering place of the ships against Troy; where Iphigeneia was to be sacrificed.

BRAURON, place in Attica, site of a sanctuary of Artemis, the final destination of Iphigeneia.

CLASHING ROCKS, or Black Rocks, at the entrance to the Black Sea.

CLYTEMNESTRA, daughter of Leda and Tyndareos, wife and murderer of Agamemnon, mother of Orestes and Iphigeneia, murdered by Orestes.

CYCLOPEAN, used of cities such as Mycenae and Tiryns, whose great walls were said to have been built by the Cyclopes.

CYNTHIAN, of the hill Cynthos on Delos. Hence Cynthia as a byname for Artemis.

DANAANS, the people of Danaos, i.e. Argives or Greeks; specifically, those Greeks who went to Troy.

DELOS, the sacred island where Apollo and Artemis were born.

DIKTYNNA, foreign (Cretan) name for Artemis.

DIOSCURI (Dioskouri), Kastor and Polydeukes (Pollux to the Romans), the Heavenly Twins. Sons of Leda and Zeus and/or Tyndareos, thus brothers of Helen and Clytemnestra. In Euripides, both were deified, and Kastor was the chief twin.

DIRKE, spring and river of Thebes.

ELEKTRA, daughter of Agamemnon and Clytemnestra, sister of Orestes and Iphigeneia, wife of Pylades.

EURIPOS, the strait between Boeotia, where Aulis is located, and the island of Euboia.

EUROTAS, the river of Sparta.

EUXINE, the Black Sea.

FURIES, our word for Erinyes, female avenging spirits. The Furies of his murdered mother pursued Orestes.

HALAI, place in Attica, site of the sanctuary to which the image of Artemis will be carried.

HELEN, daughter of Leda and Tyndareos (or Zeus), wife of Menelaos. Her elopement with Paris caused the Trojan War.

HIPPODAMEIA, daughter of Oinomaos, q.v.

ILION, Troy.

IO, daughter of Inachos, beloved by Zeus and persecuted by Hera.

IPHIGENEIA, daughter of Agamemnon and Clytemnestra.

KALCHAS, Agamemnon's diviner.

KARYSTIAN, of Karystos, opposite Halai and Brauron.

KASTALIAN, of the spring, Kastalia, at Pytho (Delphi).

LAERTES, father of Odysseus.

LEDA, daughter of Thestios, wife of Tyndareos, mother of Helen, Clytemnestra, and the Dioscuri.

LETO, goddess, beloved by Zeus, mother of Apollo and Artemis.

LEUKOTHEA ("White Goddess"), heroine transformed into a sea goddess.

LOXIAS, byname of Apollo.

MENELAOS, son of Atreus, brother of Agamemnon, husband of Helen.
MYCENAE, city in the territory of Argos.

NAUPLIA, city in the territory of Argos.
NEREID, a sea nymph or sea goddess, one of the fifty daughters of
    Nereus. The most famous was Thetis.
NEREUS, sea god, father of the fifty Nereids.

ODYSSEUS, hero of the *Odyssey*, in Euripides, Agamemnon's right-
    hand man.
OINOMAOS, king of Pisa, father (some said lover) of Hippodameia, the
    perilous princess. Her suitors had to attempt to escape with her
    in a chariot. Oinomaos would pursue, overtake, and kill them,
    until he was brought to his doom by Pelops and his own treach-
    erous charioteer and treacherous daughter.
ORESTES, son of Agamemnon and Clytemnestra.

PALAIMON, deified son of Leukothea.
PAN, god of flocks and shepherds, inventor and master of musical
    pipes.
PARNASSOS, the great mountain above Delphi (Pytho).
PELEUS, Thessalian king, mortal married to the divine Thetis, father
    of Achilles.
PELOPS, heroic ancestor of Orestes and Iphigeneia.
PHINEUS, hero plagued by the Harpies.
PHOCIANS, the people of Phocis.
PHOCIS, country adjoining Delphi, kingdom of Strophios and Pylades.
PHOIBOS (Phœbus), byname of Apollo.
PISA, country of Olympia, kingdom of Oinomaos.
POSEIDON, god of the sea.
PYLADES, son of Strophios, cousin and steadfast friend of Orestes.
PYTHIAN, of Pytho (Delphi).

SPARTA, in legend, kingdom of Tyndareos and Menelaos.
STROPHIOS, brother-in-law of Agamemnon, father of Pylades, king of
    Phocis.

TANTALOS, father of Pelops, founder of the line.
TAURIANS, people of the Crimea, whose land is not quite correctly
    called Tauris.
TAURÓPOLOS, epithet of Artemis at Halai.

THEMIS, ancient goddess, ousted from the Delphic oracle by Apollo.

THETIS, Nereid, married to the mortal Peleus; mother of Achilles.

THOAS, "the swift," king of the Taurians.

THYESTES, brother of Atreus, who quarreled with him.

TITANS, the generation of gods before the Olympians, overthrown by them.

TYNDAREOS, king of Sparta, husband of Leda, father or putative father of Helen, Clytemnestra, and the Dioscuri.